PAUL HUGHES

The British Tradition

Simpson — a World of Style

A Winning Streak: One of Max Hoff's first
advertisements for Simpsons, 1936.

The British Tradition

Simpson — a World of Style

David Wainwright

Foreword by HRH The Duke of Edinburgh

Quiller Press
London

The author gratefully acknowledges the help of many members of the staff of the DAKS Simpson Group and of Simpson Piccadilly, past and present, who have generously given him their cooperation in the writing of this book.

DW, East Molesey, Surrey, 1996.

First published 1996 by
Quiller Press Ltd
46 Lillie Road SW6 1TN

ISBN 1 899163 15 8

Designed by Tim Jaques FCSD

Produced by
Hugh Tempest Radford *Book Producers*

Printed and bound in Great Britain
by Clifford Press Ltd, Coventry

CONTENTS

The blazer in the Bentley. The Simpson design
for the Bentley Drivers Club

The style sources from the *Gentleman's Tailor and Magazine of Fashion*. For Simeon Simpson's customers there would have been (l to r) morning coat, travelling Ulster, dress jacket suit (the latter-day dinner jacket); evening dress ('tails'); golfing; walking and sports outfits. Dated 1910, they have their origins in the 1840s and were to provide inspiration for the next hundred and fifty years.

The Pivot Sleeve Golfing Jacket.

By some lucky chance, Simpson Piccadilly is celebrating the 60th anniversary of its founding in the same year that the Duke of Edinburgh's Award Scheme is celebrating the 40th anniversary of its founding. The connection is that Simpson Piccadilly has been a generous supporter of the Award Scheme for many years; it is a Shield Holder and its parent company, DAKS Simpson Group Plc, is a Charter Member.

I am therefore delighted to offer my warmest congratulations and good wishes to Simpson Piccadilly on its Diamond Jubilee and I hope it will enjoy many more anniversaries in the future.

INTRODUCTION

O n 29 April 1936 a great new store opened in London's most famous thoroughfare, Piccadilly, within a bow-shot of Eros in Piccadilly Circus, then 'the heart of Empire'.

It was a store uncompromisingly modern, and yet a building with a modernity that is timeless: simple, straightforward, confident, and sitting easily beside its older decorated companions.

From its opening, Simpson Piccadilly was recognised as one of the great stores of London. At first, it was a men's store: but within a year of opening, the true style and fashion of the clothing offered there, the evidence of quality demonstrated within, appealed equally to the discerning woman, and women's clothes and accessories were soon added.

Simpson Piccadilly was the concept of one remarkable man: Alexander Simpson, then in his early thirties, a man of his time. He was the inheritor of one of the great British tailoring businesses, created by his father over the previous forty years. He enriched his inheritance by catching the spirit of the time: enlisting new architecture, new materials, new fabrics, new ideas for display, marketing and advertising, and assembling them together in one remarkable store. It was courageous: a triumph of the brilliant management of innovation.

Sixty years later, Simpson Piccadilly is still up-to-date, fresh, exhilarating, and offering its customers the best of its time: a great store, famous round the world, still faithful to a notable tradition, but never fearing to explore the challenges of the future.

The famous Simpson Christmas tree of lights on the Piccadilly facade, designed by Natasha Kroll in the 1950s.

1

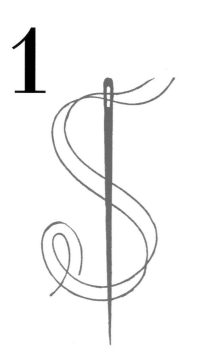

THE HOUSE OF SIMPSON

The new store - Simpson Piccadilly - emerged from a great tradition. Yet the House of Simpson, though by the 1930s a leading name in quality British tailoring, had reached that position in less than half a century.

It was in 1894 that a young man named Simeon rented a room in Middlesex Street, the boundary of the City of London and the East End. Only 16, he had the confidence, self-assurance and skill to set up his own business as a bespoke tailor. There is no question of his skill. He had the eye of an artist (it is said that he could draw straight lines and regular curves freehand), allied to the energy and imagination of an entrepreneur. Evidently he had been well taught (it is almost certain that his father was a tailor, one of the many who lived and worked in that area). Middlesex Street was better known by its nickname of Petticoat Lane, being a centre for the garment trade; on Sunday mornings the street filled with stalls selling many types of goods, but specially second-hand clothes and ready-made suits and trousers.

Simeon soon earned a reputation for the quality of his tailoring, and as his business expanded he took on staff to help him. He taught them as he had been taught. He accepted only the highest standards of craftsmanship, but he was always concerned about the conditions in which his people worked, and in consequence created a team whose members stayed with him for life.

It happened that at just this time, at the turn of the new century, the world of tailoring was being revolutionised. Machinery was taking over from traditional hand-work. The sewing-machine had been introduced (from America) in the mid-century; but when Simeon was starting his business yet more substantial new technologies were being introduced. In particular, the band-knife - powered first by gas and then electricity - enabled many thicknesses of cloth to be cut simultaneously. Machinery became available for making buttonholes, and for pressing. Simeon understood the importance of these technical advances. Tailoring was no longer solely a matter of individual craft-work; it was becoming possible to produce quality tailoring in quantity, using factory production-line methods. It was Simeon's genius to employ these new methods of production, while upholding the highest standards of quality founded in the best tradition of British tailoring.

He prospered as a result. By the age of 21 he had married, and within a few years his family was increased by two sons (Samuel in 1900, and Alexander in 1902) and a daughter (Rebecca, who married a City solicitor, Arthur Woolf). Simeon opened factories, one in Cutler Street (off Middlesex Street) and then a second, further north (in Shacklewell Lane, Stoke Newington), and then a third, in Middlesex Street itself. No sooner was a new factory started than

Simeon Simpson.

business expanded yet further. The business was expanding at such a rate because Simeon had long since realised that the future of his business lay in raising the quality of ready-to-wear tailoring so that it would be as acceptable as bespoke. He was cultivating more and more sales outlets, throughout Britain and even abroad.

The outfitting trade was divided rigorously then into two areas: men's and boys', and women's and girls'. It was further divided into the 'bespoke' trade, and ready-to-wear. No professional man or businessman would consider ready-to-wear, which was usually sold from market stalls and barrows. Even the smallest town had a gentlemen's tailor, whose workroom was usually behind the shop, which would be stacked with bales of cloth. On the arrival of a customer, the tailor would emerge in his shirt-sleeves and waistcoat, tape-measure round his neck, to conduct a civilised discussion on local affairs before measuring his client for a new suit.

But this was changing, and Simeon Simpson was helping to change it. He did not believe that ready-to-wear need be of poor quality. He observed the success of the multiple stores, many of them based in the north of England but spreading throughout the country. Often their goods were displayed on rails outside the shop, or packed together in the open windows: not only men's suits, but overcoats, trousers and shirts. All were marked with clear, hard-sell price tickets.

Under this pressure, a number of provincial bespoke tailors recognised the way the trade was changing, and began to move into this market. They increased their stock to offer greater variety, and they began to advertise. Some of the multiple stores offered a bespoke service. Simeon Simpson also offered his provincial 'customers' or agents (as they became) a bespoke service. It was remarkably efficient and reliable, since it allowed for a nearly complete suit to be sent out to the provincial tailor for a 'try-on' by the customer: the shoulders, collar, sleeves and cuffs would be 'baisted' (that is, tacked in place). The tailor would then chalk minor changes, and return the suit to Simpsons for finishing - and all within little more than a week. However, if necessary, with simple measurements, and no try-on, a suit could be ordered, completed, despatched and received in the provinces within 24 hours.

These achievements, of course, relied on excellent transport services. Up to 100 parcels were taken at 11pm each night to the main-line stations to be put on the night trains to the country. Orders for weddings and funerals were manufactured and despatched within a day. The morning mail would be collected at 6 am, and by the time most of the factory staff (the great majority men in those days) arrived for work at 8, the appropriate cloth was on the cutting room table, and shortly after 9 would be on the factory floor. Each of these orders was the responsibility of a 'chaser' who would keep track of its progress to make sure that it was finished and in the warehouse ready for despatch that evening.

By 1917, as the Great War reached its final year, the House of Simpson was one of the great successes of British men's tailoring. Simeon Simpson had to consider his family succession. His elder son, Samuel, was achieving remarkable academic success at Westminster City School, and was determined to become a doctor (an ambition he triumphantly achieved). So it was agreed that he would not join the business. But Simeon's younger son, Alexander, assuredly wanted to. At the age of 15, one year younger than his father had been when he started the business in one room in Middlesex Street, he left school and joined the business.

From the first, he was given no privileges. Like any other young apprentice, he worked his way through the factory, learning each and every aspect of the tailoring business. He learnt to evaluate and select cloth, he learnt cutting and sewing, finishing, and all other trades. He learnt marketing and (a new aspect of business in the 1920s) advertising. His father encouraged him to travel up and down the country; and then he travelled widely throughout Europe and the United States, all the time studying new techniques of manufacture and selling.

In the 1920s, men's wear had begun to change with patterns of work, and the increase in leisure. In the craft trades, the leather apron, flannel shirt, weskit and corduroys had given way to overalls. In the professions, the morning coat and top hat (though still the uniform for the City of London) was beginning to be replaced by the three-piece suit. The high standards guaranteed by Simpsons meant that more men could be fitted 'off-the-peg', with ready-to-wear suits. Increased leisure meant that special clothing was being created for sports wear: the Prince of Wales, a keen golfer, was also an inventive dresser, wearing 'plus fours' and Fair Isle sweaters, and introducing the windowpane 'Prince of Wales check'.

The success of the House of Simpson was such that the various factories were stretched to overflowing. With his father's approval and support, Alec Simpson began to plan a large factory in Stoke Newington where all manufacturing could be centralised efficiently. The factory in Stoke Newington - steel-framed - was opened in 1929, and all the work of the business was concentrated there, in a building that was regarded throughout the trade as the most advanced of its day. Alec Simpson planned the layout with scrupulous care, paying particular attention to good lighting. There were showrooms, a range of administrative offices, and a high standard of welfare facilities including a canteen where workers could obtain good food at a cheap price.

One result was that in the financial crisis that devastated world economies from 1929 and into the 1930s, the House of Simpson was much less severely threatened than many other companies. The general trend towards ready-to-wear was in the spirit of the times: but many were willing to pay for quality, since customers sought clothes that would last. Soon after it was opened, the Stoke Newington factory had to be substantially enlarged because of increased demand. Simeon and Alec Simpson faced the 1930s with understandable optimism.

Tailors in the new Stoke Newington factory in the early 1930s. The hand sewing is traditional but the environment is revolutionary, well lit and hygenic. The tailoring workroom display was a very popular attraction in Simpson Piccadilly.

2 THE IDEA OF A GREAT STORE

The new Stoke Newington factory.

*I*n the spring of 1932 Alec Simpson was perfecting his new invention in men's wear. He was a keen sportsman (as a boy he had boxed in the East End boys' clubs, in his twenties he turned out regularly for the Simpson Social Club football team at Stoke Newington). As he approached 30, he took up golf; soon he shared the irritation that golfers felt when they were impeded by braces: following the swing, the shirt would ride up. There must, Alec decided, be a better way of constructing sports trousers. Being Alec Simpson, he pursued the problem until he had solved it.

Solve it, he certainly did. The answer was a trouser tailored to the waist, and held in place by rubber pads sewn into the waistband. Having arranged for samples to be manufactured in quantity, until he achieved trousers that satisfied his high standards, he turned to the question of marketing. He was prepared to charge a high price for quality, and set the retail price at 30 shillings a pair. He recognised perfectly well that this would be seen as expensive in the trade (when at this time one firm was named the 'Fifty Shilling Tailors', since they would provide a complete suit for that price). To ask 30 shillings for a single pair of trousers - the equivalent of £40 in 1990s prices - might be considered foolhardy by Simpson's main customers, the men's outfitters in the provinces. But Alec Simpson was confident that he knew his market.

One of his provincial customers, Dudley Beck, had become a trusted business associate. Dudley Beck was the head of an up-market family firm of men's outfitters in Chester: to Alec Simpson, he was not only a good customer, but a personal friend and a reliable touchstone of what the trade would accept and find saleable. One evening, Alec Simpson sat down with Beck in a brainstorming session to devise a name - a name that would sell - for these new trousers. The two of them threw various combinations of letters to and fro - and eventually devised a short list. They wanted a short, snappy name that would catch the eye and remain in the mind. It is said that they started to experiment with variations on their own names: DB and AS . . . would make 'DABS' . . . No, too soft, fishy . . . But try the last letter of Beck's name . . . DK and AS . . . would make 'DAKS' . . . The session had lasted into the small hours; nevertheless, in the middle of the night, Alec Simpson telephoned his advertising agent, Bill Crawford, and began reading to him the list of potential names. Woken from sleep, Crawford listened, and then hearing one name, he said: 'You've got it. DAKS: yes - it has overtones of "dad" and "slacks": reliability, and comfort. That's the one. And now - goodnight!'

The British patent for DAKS - No. 386871 - was registered on 9th June 1932, and in the years immediately following in Australia, Italy, USA, Holland, Canada, Denmark, Norway, Belgium, France, South Africa,

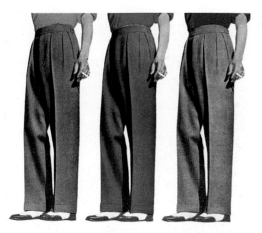

Now in 41 colours and 8 materials

Keep up-to-date with your collection! Ask for the 1936 Daks Colour Chart showing the whole range in full colour. All Daks 30/-, Daks Shorts 21/-. From all good men's shops, or write Simpson, 202, Piccadilly, London.

DAKS

Classic DAKS, 1936. The patent waistband ensured ease and security.

Switzerland and Sweden. More countries followed later. The trousers were first made in a factory specially rented in Shepperton Road, until a further extension could be built at Stoke Newington: such was Simpson's confidence, he ordered 100,000 pairs to be manufactured ahead of the launch.

*   *   *

Then, while Alec Simpson was planning the great advertising campaign to launch DAKS, he suffered a crushing personal blow. His father Simeon Simpson, the founder of the firm, died at the age of 54. The shock was devastating for Alec, who found himself managing director of the House of Simpson at the age of 30. His father Simeon had taught him the trade, while building the family company into one of the most successful firms in British menswear manufacturing. Probate was granted to his two sons, though the younger, Alexander, was named first - no doubt as the senior and executive director of the family business. Simeon Simpson's personal estate was valued at £80,244 (1990s equivalent, about £2 million).

*   *   *

Alec Simpson had no doubt that the best way he could honour his father's memory was by continuing the expansion of the business. So, pausing only to commission a portrait plaque of his father for the entrance hall of the Stoke Newington factory, he continued with the planning to launch DAKS. The inimitable trade mark, designed at Crawfords by Ashley Havinden, was registered in Britain in November 1933, and throughout that year and 1934, a substantial newspaper advertising campaign was launched throughout Britain, using the slogan 'Comfort in action'. The sales pitch was very deliberately linked with the provincial outfitters who had become such good customers of Simpson, and the local ads always mentioned the local shops where DAKS were on sale.

A typical advertisement appeared in PUNCH, the humorous magazine then high fashion (and carrying some of the first colour advertising in the British media), in April 1934.

* the slacks for cracks!

DAKS

The most beautiful trousers you have ever seen - with all the improvements you have always wanted. Cut to hang straight from the hips and leave your limbs free. No braces or belt needed. Soft pads of porous rubber that won't let your shirt ride up. Superbly tailored in a specially woven worsted flannel, light as silk and cool as cambric. In crisp clear greys, oatmeal, blue-grey, intense white, and chalk stripes. Price 30/- a pair.

Stocked by all leading outfitters in every town in the United Kingdom and Northern Ireland. If you cannot get Daks, write to DAKS, 233 High Holborn, London WC1.

The only comfort-in-action trousers.

(The address was that of the advertising agency, Crawfords.)
It may be that someone decided that men would not, after all, be attracted to 'the most beautiful trousers'; in the next published version of this ad, the opening sales pitch changed to: 'The *grandest* trousers you have ever seen.'

Advertising was becoming increasingly powerful in the 1920s and 1930s, and Alec Simpson was strongly convinced of its value. He

The success of the century

It's no exaggeration. At one time, really practical slacks for games just did not exist. Then along came Daks, with their comfort-in-action cut, superb hang and neat shirt control. And what happened? Crack sportsmen — not to mention some half-a-million other men, took to them with enthusiasm. Australian Test Teams have worn Daks since 1934 – and they're wearing them again this year. Have you ever tried on a pair of Daks? If not—go and do so. First you'll need some Daks greys. But ask to see the Daks chart, and have a look at the cool tropicals, crisp linens, the rough stuffs, corduroys, and all the forty-one colours and eight materials. 30/- a pair from all good men's shops, or write Simpson, 202 Piccadilly, W.1.

Clothes for cricket, 1937. Simpson were responsible for dressing many teams and players, throughout the years...

WOMEN'S
DAKS

the

perfect

slacks

hasn't taken good players long to discover that Women's Daks from Simpson, Piccadilly, are the perfect golf slacks. The neat fit at the waist and comfort-in-action cut gives you a new sense of freedom. The faultless hang makes you look so slim and professional. In grey flannels, crisp linens, and most of the forty-one Daks colours and light materials. 30/- a pair.

and to complete the picture :
poplin shirt, in lots of colours, with riding tail that buttons under and makes undies superfluous, 10/6.
aero-spun scarf 3/6.
light, soft summer golf shoes of unlined fairway calf, with Scottish craftsmanship plus American elegance, 45/-.
poplin sun cap 12/9.
to be found, together with the most exciting tennis, beach and street clothes, on the 4th Floor.

Simpson, 202 Piccadilly, W.1 (Regent 20

The lady golfer, 1938. An ultra functional outfit with the slacks worn with a shirt combination obviating underwear and a new style sun cap.

particularly relied on Bill Crawford, who (not least because he was the same age as Alec's father Simeon) became something of a father-figure. Crawford was an enthusiast for things modern and new. His office in Holborn (built in 1927) was of concrete, black marble, stainless steel and glass. He often visited the United States (the home of lively advertising) and in the 1920s took on the European advertising of Chrysler cars. When, during the General Strike in 1926, communications with the continent were disrupted, a group of Crawfords' staff were sent to Antwerp to run the continental campaign from there. Because the local printers had few modern type-faces, Crawfords linked up with the Ullstein publishing and printing firm in Berlin. In 1927 - the year Bill Crawford became Sir William, for his services to British government advertising - Crawfords opened an office in Berlin, using many graphic design ideas from the great German design school, the Bauhaus. The staff were also aware of the new department stores being designed in several German cities by the architect Erich Mendelsohn. Thus one of Alec Simpson's closest advisers in the early 1930s was involved with, and using, the most important ideas in modern design and advertising in both America and Germany.

A highly important showcase for the men's fashion trade at this period was the British Industries Fair, a great bonanza of an exhibition held in three centres - in Earls Court and the White City in London, and also in Birmingham. The menswear section was at the White City (the exhibition hall was on the site of the present BBC Television Centre). At the BIF held in February 1934, Alec Simpson made a breakthrough. He took a far larger display stand than anyone else, and on it Crawfords designed a series of 'stage sets', each one representing the background for a particular sport - golf, cricket, riding, sailing, and so forth. Alec Simpson hired a small army of male models, and they moved around their setting miming the appropriate game - each of them dressed in Simpson-tailored sports clothes. The stand was a famous advertising success, the first time anyone had got away from the tradition of showing clothing on static lay figures, and the White City display became known in the trade as 'Alec Simpson's show'. Of course, DAKS were in the forefront.

At one of the official luncheons during the BIF at the White City, the President of the Board of Trade, Walter Runciman, said: 'Britain's fashions in men's clothes lead the world, and I hope they will always do so. When some of my foreign friends come to London from America or Europe they always have in their programmes a number of visits to Savile Row; and that is only one indication of the position that we, as makers of men's clothes, hold in the world.'

Alec Simpson would have echoed that sentiment, not least because (it is said) as a boy his great ambition was to order a hand-tailored suit from one of the famous names at the most distinguished peak of his trade, one of the greats of Savile Row. Once he was running his own business, his aim was to achieve Savile Row standards in the ready-made ranges that had become the foundation of Simpson's success.

But in 1934, there was nowhere in central London, near Savile Row, where those foreign visitors could go to examine and buy exclusively Simpson clothes and the increasingly successful DAKS (the pessimists in the trade who predicted that few people would pay 30s for a pair of trousers were soon proved totally wrong, as the month-on-month sales figures proved).

LACKS AND SHORTS FOR ALL THE SPORTS

WHITES

Worsted-flannel or gabardine. At Wimbledon last year the
Americans hiked gabardine. The conservative Englishman
stuck to their flannels. Answer — both are good!

SPORTS SHORTS

Out to be comfortable — without being conspicuous.
Really tough in corduroy. Cool as a cucumber in linen.
But you can have them in any of the Daks materials!

DAKS

No need to cramp your style by confining yourself to one pair of Daks this year! We've translated Daks comfort-in-
action into a galaxy of materials and colours. To begin with the unusual; Corduroy Daks, beige to brown. Navy
blue — in worsted flannel, linen and tweed. Smoke white and biscuit linens. Smooth whipcords — and 'rough stuffs'
for hard going. Then, your choice of greys is legion — there are Air Force blue, brown and lovat Daks. And whites,

Sports wear, always a popular department, but
elitist or aspirational in 1938 with whites at 30
shillings and shorts at a guinea.

Alec Simpson.

So the thought entered Alec Simpson's mind that he would build a great
store at the heart of London. His rival, of his father's generation, Austin
Reed, had done that a decade earlier. The trade had predicted that Reed, by
abandoning his City base in Fenchurch Street and opening a large store for
menswear in the West End in the 1920s, was never going to succeed. He
had succeeded: and now Alec Simpson prepared to open his own West End
store - but bigger and better, more modern than the one in Regent Street.
In his tours of Europe and the United States he had visited most of the
great retail stores - particularly those built in Chicago in the 1880s and
1890s by the American architect Louis H Sullivan (who coined the
catchphrase of the modern movement in architecture and design, 'Form
follows function' - buildings and industrial artifacts should visually, and in
their use of materials, reflect their function, and not be disguised by
unnecessary decoration). Sullivan also designed one of the first great
American steel-framed towers, the Wainwright Building in St Louis (1890-
1). Alec Simpson also knew and admired the Schocken department stores
built in Germany in the 1920s.

So, after the success of the Simpson stand at the British Industries Fair,
Alec Simpson began to search for a possible shop site in central London.
Early in spring 1935 the Commissioners of Crown Lands announced that
the site of the old Geological Museum in Piccadilly was to be sold on a
building lease, for 99 years from April 5th 1935. The contents of the
Museum had been removed, some time before, to the national exhibition
campus at South Kensington. The existing building had to be demolished,
and replaced by 'shops, offices, chambers or other business premises
and/or for the erection of a cinematograph or other theatre' (this was the
heyday of the picture palaces). The site had a frontage of 71 feet to
Piccadilly and to Jermyn Street, and a ground area of about 11,000 square
feet. A clothing store in Piccadilly would be very appropriate. For the name
is said to be derived from the Dutch *Pikedillekens*: scraps, or the tips or
corners of a piece of cloth. Nikolaus Pevsner says (in his *Buildings of
London*) that it was probably given the name when the street and the
circus were the tip of built-over London, before it began to spread east at
the beginning of the 17th century.

Alec Simpson went along to the London Auction Mart on 27th March
1935; and by the end of the afternoon he was the owner of the lease of the
'old Geological Museum site', from 5th April, with a bid of £11,000 (in
1990s prices, about £250,000). He was committed to provide a building with
elevations to the public streets that were of 'handsome architectural
design', and 'faced in Portland stone approved by the Commissioners'.

On 5th April 1935, the first day Alec Simpson was entitled by law to call
himself leaseholder of the Piccadilly site, he wrote to his architect, Joseph
Emberton:

> I know that now we have got to work damnably fast, but it is absolutely
> imperative that we have the ground floor finished for September 1st. I know
> this is a hell of a job, but we just must accomplish it.
>
> I should be awfully grateful if in the next few days you would work out a
> schedule diary of procedure, so that we can check ourselves from time to
> time as to how we are getting on.
>
> With kindest regards, I am
> Yours very sincerely
> A. Simpson

Joseph Emberton.

He was determined to demolish a substantial stone building, and design, erect and stock a large store in its place, in less than five months. Fortunately Joseph Emberton, the architect, was of a calm disposition (though he earned a reputation of being a hard employer: there was a high turnover of staff in his office, few assistants staying with him for long). He had come from the Black Country, and had qualified at night school before moving to London - to the Royal College of Art and the Royal Academy Schools. He served his apprenticeship designing stands for the great British Empire Exhibition at Wembley in 1924, and then in 1927 a much admired exhibition for the Advertising Association. His best qualification for designing a new store was, ironically, that he had designed the interior of Austin Reed's in Regent Street. He was earning a reputation as a 'modern' architect: his work at the Royal Corinthian Yacht Club, Burnham, had already won him the RIBA Bronze Medal. He wrote articles on store design, admiring Bonwit Tellers in New York, the Wanamaker Building in Philadelphia, the Galeries Lafayette in Paris, and particularly the modern stores designed in Germany by Erich Mendelsohn for the Schocken Department Stores, in Nuremberg, Stuttgart and Chemnitz (the last, with its bands of windows, was built in 1928 and is clearly an influence on Simpsons).

In 1935 Emberton was 46 - middle-aged compared with his 32-year-old client Mr Simpson (in the letters they wrote to each other, sometimes almost daily, during the building of Simpson Piccadilly they almost invariably addressed each other - from start to finish - as 'Dear Mr Emberton' and 'Dear Mr Simpson', in the formal custom of professional men of the time).

The main elements of the store as it stands today, sixty years later, were clearly established from the first: the great bands of window on Piccadilly and Jermyn Street; the vertical window rising floor to ceiling by the immense central marble staircase, providing daylight to the midst of each floor; the unimpeded open floors, from front to back; the non-reflecting concave windows at street level - all these were among the first ideas proposed by Emberton, and immediately agreed by Alec Simpson. Five days after the 'start', on 5th April, Alec Simpson sent a sketch of the Piccadilly frontage, proposing a recessed curve at pavement level 'to draw the public into the store'; his pencil sketch, at this very early stage, shows the strips of windows between white panels (of Portland stone), which had evidently been agreed between client and architect already. He did not get his curved entrance, because it would have meant abandoning the non-reflecting windows (which Emberton was insistent upon).

A few days later, Alec Simpson was tackling essentials: 'I think that it is so important for us to get down to what we are going to sell and how we are going to sell it . . .' Emberton noted that Simpson intended to advertise for a 'men's outfitter man', whom he would send to Germany and America with the store's first Manager, W P Yates - he was another Simpson 'customer', who having been running his family's large store in Bradford, had been persuaded to come to London.

In May, the tenders for demolishing the old building had come in: Goodman, Price would do the job in six weeks, or eight if they were not allowed to work at night. Alec Simpson agreed that the building would be built as high as permitted, to exploit the site to the maximum. At various times he thought of letting the upper floors as flats, or as offices; but gradually he came round to the idea that Simpson would occupy the whole building.

When at the end of June, Emberton was asked by the London County

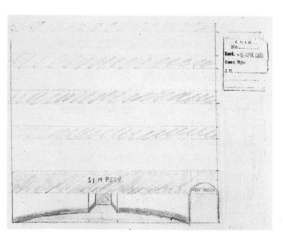

This sketch by Alexander Simpson of his ideas for the Piccadilly facade was sent to the architect Joseph Emberton on 9th April 1935 - which indicates that before demolition work had even started on the former building on the site, client and architect were already agreed on the main elements of the new building.

A letterhead received by the architect from Alexander Simpson at Stoke Newington in July 1935, which indicates how Emberton, by doodling in pencil and lengthening the tail of the 'p' in 'Simpson' was starting the creative process that produced the now familiar logo of Simpson Piccadilly.

Ashley Script, designed by Ashley Havinden.

Council for written evidence that he was the 'authorised agent' of Simpsons, he realised that he had been given no written contract; and he wrote to Alec asking for written confirmation of their agreement that Emberton would be paid a fee of 5,000 guineas for the building, and 500 guineas for the shopfitting (1990s values: about £150,000). Simpson sent the confirmation, with the comment: 'Please forgive me for not having confirmed our agreement. Just the same it is very nice to think that there has been so much mutual trust and understanding that we have got so far without ever having put into writing the terms of the appointment.'

By this stage Simpson had realised that his intention of opening the ground floor on 1st September (presumably while the builders were still banging away on the upper floors) was not practicable, and a new opening date of 1st March 1936 had been agreed. He was still worrying about details. Would three lifts really be adequate? Were they really big enough? Could one break through the basement wall and supply the snack bar from the teashop next door (he would write to his friend Salmon of J.Lyons)?

And if 'Mr Ashley', of Crawfords, be asked to collaborate in lettering the name Simpson for Piccadilly, 'it would be as well for this to be got on with at once, as this same lettering should be incorporated in making outdoor signs for our agents throughout the country.' This is the first mention of Ashley Havinden, who was to contribute much to Simpson Piccadilly, and also to become one of the leading British graphic designers, and a Royal Designer for Industry. He had joined Crawfords, the advertising agency, at the age of 19 - and though largely untrained, had demonstrated a remarkable flair for graphics and illustration. He had been responsible for the DAKS newspaper advertising campaign: now he was to provide Simpson Piccadilly with its script alphabet (soon produced as a printing typeface by Monotype called 'Ashley') used throughout the store for 60 years, remaining fresh and vigorous as ever.

Most important in that letter was Alec Simpson's insistence that the 'house style' of Simpson Piccadilly should be carried through into 'outdoor signs for our agents throughout the country'. It was Alec Simpson's idea, and fundamental to the creation of the great store, that it should be a London base for the provincial outfitters who were selling Simpson tailoring, and now DAKS.

London attracted more visitors than usual in the summer of 1935, for on 6th May King George V celebrated his Jubilee, and to mark his 25 years on the throne he and Queen Mary drove round the capital to the cheers of their people. The great Cunard liner, named after Queen Mary, entered service on the Atlantic crossing that year, taking under five days from Southampton to New York.

On 17th July 1935 Simpson (Piccadilly) Limited was formed as a Private Company, with Alexander Simpson as sole Director, and with a substantial financial loan from Barclays Bank. In the summer of 1935, while the store was still little more than a rumour in the trade, Alec Simpson wrote a 'Memorandum to all Simpson Customers, Announcing the Opening of SIMPSON, PICCADILLY, London's Greatest Men's Wear Store'. (The 'Customers', in this case, were the provincial retailers using the House of Simpson as their wholesaler.) The document is extraordinary in its openness: not many businessmen, at any period, would so frankly admit that what they were creating was, for the foreseeable future, going to trade at a loss:

One hundred yards from Piccadilly Circus, and with a wide frontage on

The controversial and advanced steelwork, designed by Felix Samuely during the construction of Simpson Piccadilly, 1935.

Piccadilly itself, there will rise during the next year a great new, and modern, men's store - planned by Simpson, owned by Simpson, controlled throughout by Simpson, bearing the name of Simpson. There is probably no finer shopsite than this in the entire world. Certainly, no store devoted exclusively to men's wear has ever occupied so commanding and exceptional position. Added to which, 'Simpson, Piccadilly' will unquestionably be the largest men's wear store in London and probably the largest of its kind in the world.

The project is extremely costly. It is so costly, indeed, that Simpson cannot hope, and are not hoping, to derive any profit whatsoever from its actual trading - at least for several years. Yet, every detail from start to finish has been planned with a firm intention, deliberate care and cool judgement.

Alec Simpson addressed his country 'customers' as 'Partners in Progress'. He promised them that the new store in Piccadilly would offer itself as their London headquarters. It would not only stock the complete ranges of DAKS and other Simpson-tailored clothes, but its marketing would be supported by a huge nationwide advertising campaign that would be designed to attract business not only to Simpson Piccadilly, but also to the country outfitters who were stocking Simpson tailoring.

There would be other attractions. There was to be a club-room, which would welcome the provincial outfitters when they came to London; they would be actively encouraged to use it as their London base. The best display styles would be used in the store - and offered to 'Partners in Progress'. Their assistants in training would be welcome to spend time in the store.

Alec Simpson summed up his policy in launching the new store:

1. Simpsons are going to maintain and increase public respect for well-tailored, well-styled 'quality' clothes.

2. Simpsons are going to undertake a nation-wide advertising campaign, as heavy as those campaigns which are at present lowering the prices and status of men's tailoring.

3. We are going to identify Simpson clothes in the minds of all men with west end standards of quality and cut, by opening the greatest men's wear store in the west end.

4. Without detracting from, but rather strengthening your individual business, we are going to provide you with a vastly more valuable Simpson agency, an organisation second-to-none, and a great London store which is virtually your own.

In this forthright document Alec Simpson set down his credo – evidently drafted by his own hand, though no doubt checked through by his adviser Bill Crawford for its public relations and advertising aspects. In general, some in the trade considered the idea bold and imaginative: but provincial retailers and the trade as a whole (in the years following the great depression and mass unemployment) reacted to such innovations with considerable cynicism. Alec Simpson was unabashed. He intended that Simpson Piccadilly was to be 'a great new, and modern, men's store'.

With the aid of his architect, Joseph Emberton, the store was to be modern in its use of materials. Today, it is difficult for the casual shopper to appreciate just how 'modern' Simpson Piccadilly was, in its use of materials that were innovative (and to many people, strange) in the mid-1930s. One contemporary who was not frightened of innovative materials was at this time working as a fitter in the Royal Air Force, preparing the supermarine seaplane to take part in an international air race. At that time known as 'Aircraftman Shaw', he had earned fame years earlier as T E Lawrence, 'Lawrence of Arabia'.(The aircraft he was servicing was a few years later to be transformed into one of the great planes of the Battle of Britain, the Supermarine Spitfire.) Lawrence was enthused by new materials: a friend recalled 'how often he mentioned stainless steel, chromium plate, and zip fasteners; the cleanliness of the two former, and the efficiency of the last, appealed to him. He said what beautiful things the world contained, in the way of materials. Steel. Unpainted woods. Bakelite. Coloured glass . . .'

Simpson Piccadilly is structurally a steel-framed building, and has won awards for its quality (the steel framing was so novel - devised by the leading structural engineer, another German emigré, Felix Samuely - that the London County Council, having delayed planning approval for some weeks, refused it: a number of girders, specially made for the building, and already installed, had to be taken out and replaced). Many of the shop fittings were natural woods. There is much chromium-plate in the building - most dramatically, in the core of the immense light-fitting, 90 feet high, that at night illuminates the great central staircase. Yet chromium-plating had been introduced commercially less than 10 years earlier (taken up largely by the motor trade). The zip fastener had been around since the 1890s in America, but only in the late '20s and early '30s were they introduced to men's and women's clothing. The generous use of glass - clear, not coloured - was a feature of much forward-looking architecture of the time, well demonstrated in the great bands of windows at Simpson Piccadilly. 'Bakelite' was a trade

Night work at Simpson Piccadilly, viewed from Jermyn Street through to the colonnade of the old Piccadilly Hotel, from the painting by Vincent Evans, 1935.

Fitting a new style at the Stoke Newington factory in the 1930s.

name for one of the first commercial plastics. Substitute 'plastics' in T E Lawrence's list, and one recognises just how perceptive he was about new materials - as were the imaginative businessmen who took the risk of using them: men such as Alexander Simpson.

At the end of August, Alec Simpson produced a list of stock he intended to carry, so that his architect could start planning the interior. He kept his executive staff at Stoke Newington working on it until 11.30 one night (he noted on the letter).

CLOTHING

Lounge suits	Minimum 10,000 (allow for 12,000)
Overcoats	2,000 (3,000 winter,1 Sept-30 Jan)
Raincoats	800

DRESS WEAR

Dinner suits	600
Full dress suits	700
Dress overcoats	120, and space for skeleton stock of dress vests, shirts, collars and ties.

SPORTS CLOTHING

Flannel trousers	4,000 pairs
Shorts	240 pairs
Plus fours	Odd plus fours 250 prs
Sports jackets	1200
Golf suits	700
Flannel suits	(Jackets and trousers) 900
Golf blouses	350
Riding clothes	Breeches and Jodpurs together 500 pairs
Tattersall vests	100
	Note: There must be a dummy horse in the fitting rooms to try the breeches.

FORMAL CLOTHES

Morning coats and vests	400
Black jackets & waistcoats	600
Stripe trousers	1,000
Wedding vests	100

TROPICAL WEAR

As yet we know nothing about this. We do note, however, that in addition to the suitable tropical clothing we must also stock the type of furniture these people carry around with them . . .

HATS

Hats	In all, 2,250
Caps	500

SHOES

We do not yet know, but I think you [Emberton] have a very good idea of the size of a shoe department.

TAILORING

We have already given you particulars . . .

As regards stock of cloth carried, 500 suit lengths will be very ample.

Emberton has noted after the last paragraph:

Large dept - 12 fitting rooms, 20 cutters, up to 30 tailors.

Obviously Alec Simpson had a vision of the store that even 60 years later is still recognisably Simpson Piccadilly - not least the inclusion of so much leisure-wear, based on DAKS but extending into the various sports that he had included in the Simpson stand at the British Industries Fair, two years earlier.

But apart from all that, Alec Simpson was planning to have a bespoke tailoring department, fully staffed, occupying a large area of one floor, with tailors, cutters and pressers working away in full view of the customers. In mid-September he wrote to Hollister, his deputy at Stoke Newington:

> . . . Give me an absolute layout for making, by craftsmanship principles, one man, one girl per cutter and a hand presser, for Piccadilly. I want about ten pairs, and the correct number of pressers to work for these ten pairs. I want the men to sit on tables and the girls on tailors' stools. Then I want a layout for twelve bespoke cutters and eight trimmers or trouser cutters, i.e. 20 in all. The purpose of this layout is to guide Mr Emberton in making his plans to accommodate those people in the bespoke tailoring department in Piccadilly. Get these plans drawn up for Mr Emberton over the weekend, submitting them to him on Monday . . . Will you also send to Mr Emberton a suit length and a double suit length of 18oz worsted and a 3 yd length of 28oz overcoating. Also give him the dimensions of half a piece of dress coating.

Alec Simpson wrote these instructions to Stoke Newington because he was unable to be there in person. He had been feeling tired for some time, under all this pressure, and would occasionally complain of aches and pains, ascribing them to a touch of rheumatism or lumbago. So, under protest, he had agreed to go into the London Clinic for a check-up. By mid-October he was back at work, recommending Commercial Union as insurers for the new building (the Crown Commissioners approved the recommendation), debating cork vs. carpet for the general flooring (cork was chosen) and writing to Emberton: 'You are obtaining suggestions and prices from sculptors to submit to me' (it seems that Eric Gill was approached: the leading modern 'architectural' sculptor of the day, Gill had in 1931 provided the figures of Prospero and Ariel for the new Broadcasting House. Discussions took place, but were not conclusive).

As the new year dawned, it became clear that the hoped-for opening date of 1st March 1936 would never be achieved (not least because of the immense and costly problems of reorganising the steelwork, to comply with LCC planning decisions). So Alec Simpson accepted the inevitable further delay, and set a new opening date of 29th April 1936, allowing four months to complete and furnish the structure, stock it with goods, and recruit and train a staff of 300.

There was a further delay at the end of January, when the country was thrown into disarray by the death of King George V, and London was filled with visitors attending the State funeral. It was known that the new young bachelor king, Edward VIII, was a modernist, and consequently in society, modernity became fashionable among wider circles.

By this time Alec Simpson was concentrating on the display of goods, which he regarded as of immense importance. At the end of January (three months to opening) he wrote to Emberton: 'I had Moholy-Nagy down here yesterday to interview a furniture man with me, and . . . he would appreciate having drawings of all the display units throughout the building, so that he could get to work on display ideas.'

László Moholy-Nagy had come to London (via Amsterdam) as a refugee from Nazi Germany, encouraged to come by Herbert Read and Ashley Havinden. Born in Hungary, and originally trained as a lawyer, he had been director of the foundation course at the Bauhaus. The reputation of the great German design school of the 1920s, directed by the architect Walter Gropius, had spread throughout Europe and become a potent influence on

László Moholy-Nagy

the modern movement in graphics, art, architecture and industry. Moholy-Nagy had in 1928 set his Bauhaus students a project to design the layout of a modern department store selling clothing. But his interests, and his imagination, were limitless. He was a keen photographer, typographer, film-maker, experimenter with new materials (he was among the first to explore the artistic possibilities of making new shapes by heat-forming plastics, a knowledge he was to exploit at Simpsons by displaying shirts and jackets on heat-formed body shapes of transparent plastic - perhaps the first time this idea was put into practice). While in London he designed film sets for the Alexander Korda film of H G Wells's *Things to Come*, and edited a special edition of the *Architectural Review* about the British seaside, illustrated with his own colour photographs - an early use of colour photography in a British magazine (he arranged the layout and typography of that issue: Moholy-Nagy was like that). He also took the photographs and provided drawings for two classic books of 1937-38: Bernard Fergusson's *Eton Portrait*, and *An Oxford University Chest* by the young John Betjeman. He designed an aviation exhibition for Imperial Airways at the Science Museum, and posters for London Transport.

With Gropius, Mies van der Rohe and other Bauhaus veterans who spent a couple of years in Hampstead after Hitler's pogrom against the Jews, he found London too limited for his talents, moved with his wife to America in July 1937, and ending in Chicago founded his own design school, and became design consultant to several companies including the Parker Pen Company, for whom he designed the Parker 51, a design classic. On Moholy-Nagy's death in 1946 Ken Parker wrote: 'His interest in our success and welfare was such you would have thought he was the sole owner of the business . . . He was always very far in the future in his thinking. He was a stimulating mentality if ever there was one.' His influence on Simpsons at this frenzied time was considerable; and it is a credit to all involved, particularly Joseph Emberton the architect, that the introduction of this genius was assimilated with all other complications.

There certainly were problems, in the winter of 1935-36. Not the least of them was the weather. That February, there was a series of exceptionally severe frosts. The windows could not be put into the top floor, because the tiling cement on the window cills would not set in the frost. Emberton wrote to Alec Simpson: 'I am getting a little anxious about the drying out of the building . . .' Simpson replied : 'I note the trouble you mention . . . and I can only say that you must overcome it.' A few days later, Emberton invited the chief engineer from the Stoke Newington factory to attend the switching on of heat in the Piccadilly store. On the following day, Alec Simpson wrote a letter to his architect that has a distinct flavour of gritted teeth and high tension:

> Knowing that normal times and conditions have not applied at any time to the building at Piccadilly, I was not so worried as I might have been when my own Engineer informed me that the amount of electrical work still to be done was, in his opinion, so great that we would not be able to open on the 29th April. As you have never brought up the question of electrical work in delaying things I assume that you have this matter well in hand and that there is no cause for anxiety . . .

Emberton's response does not survive. There were other matters to be decided. Alec Simpson wrote to say that Moholy-Nagy had put forward a good idea for the departmental signing - perhaps, on the pillar signs by the lifts, those signs might have symbols: wines with a bottle of wine; sports department, say, with a tennis racket and golf club. Oh, and talking about

The comfort and confidence of custom tailoring but at an, almost, off-the-peg price. A Simpson advertisement of 1937 promoted the advantages of a firm in the hand tailoring tradition.

The austere facade with identification only on the ground floor, at the opening, April 1936.

The store facade with the DAKS logo.

wine, we want wine vaults in the basement. Emberton to Simpson: The LCC terms of consent refuse access by the public to the basement: and there is a clause forbidding the storage of inflammable spirit. Simpson's office to Emberton: He is of the opinion that whisky is not covered by this. Try the LCC again. (Ten days later, Customs and Excise refused to countenance wine vaults.) Simpson to Emberton: Is the size of the hors d'oeuvres trolley in the restaurant adequate?

February 21. Simpson to Emberton: We need a board room. A board table 8ft by 3ft to seat 10 people, and in this board room a desk will be required for my personal use. I want the board room furnished with the greatest simplicity and yet to look substantial and reliable. (Emberton telephoned Bath Cabinet Makers. The board room still exists, substantial and reliable, complete with three Bauhaus light fittings, white globes set in chromium mounts; the board table is also original.)

February 26. Emberton to Simpson: We are feeding in temporary electrical installations to work the ventilation plant. It is essential for the drying of the building that the ventilation plant shall be working as soon as possible . . . I have called in the Building Research Station - hot air is being pumped into the building over the weekend. The effect on the wood is unpredictable. There is uncertainty over lighting: the contractor requires two weeks to carry out wiring and erect fittings.

On the evening of *27th February* 1936 Joseph Emberton took Alec Simpson to stand on the north side of Piccadilly and look across the road at his great new store. As darkness fell, the neon light strips, red, blue and green, set above and beside the windows, began their magic ritual. Emberton had used coloured neon lights vividly in his showbiz work at the Blackpool Pleasure Beach a year or two earlier. Now he elevated the system, then brand new, to elegance and sophistication at the heart of Empire. That simple severe facade of white Portland stone and glass became, gradually, a colourful tutti-frutti of lighting effects: red, blue or green; red/blue; blue/green; red/green; and all together - red-blue-and-green, mixing to a magical, breathtaking white. Seeing all this for the first time for real, Alec Simpson was entranced.

On the next day the client wrote a personal letter to his architect.

I was positively thrilled last night and would like to take this opportunity of repeating my congratulations to you.

The lighting of the building is undoubtedly a masterpiece and its advertising value should be almost incalculable. I am indeed thankful to you for having thought of and worked out the idea so brilliantly.

Kind regards,

Yours sincerely,

A Simpson.

That joyful high was reached at a most appropriate moment. For at this critical point, three weeks before the opening of the store, Alec Simpson took a day off work, for a personal engagement. On 3rd April 1936, at West London Synagogue, he was married. His bride was Ceridwen Rees Roberts (known as Ceri), the 22-year-old daughter of his next-door neighbour in Fitzjohn's Avenue. Her father was a close friend of his parents, and also the family physician: Dr Rees-Roberts was principal witness, and another witness was Alec's elder brother, Sam, who at this time was becoming known as a distinguished physician, medical researcher and teacher. The brothers were very close, but while the elder brother took a benevolent and fraternal interest in the business, his professional life was entirely devoted

to medicine. After taking a first class degree at Cambridge (and captaining the university boxing team in 1919), he had done postgraduate research at the Mayo Clinic in the United States, the Charitée Hospital in Berlin and the Lister Institute, London - three renowned centres for medical research (in the three countries that were most important to his brother: America, Germany and Britain). By the time of his brother's wedding, Dr S Leonard Simpson was becoming known in his mid-thirties as a distinguished endocrinologist (only his family and very close friends knew him as 'Sam': professionally he used his second initial and was known as 'Leonard').

There was no time for Alec and Ceri to enjoy a honeymoon, and little time to celebrate the wedding at the grand house, Rookery Wood, he had bought for them in Highgate (commissioning Joseph Emberton to design new gates, and to supervise some building alterations).

The store was due to open in less than a month. New ideas were passed to and fro. Simpson was worried that the front canopy was too black, too bleak. The LCC refused to allow the name SIMPSON to appear on it (the local authority relented in later years): Emberton suggested window boxes with flowers, and Alec Simpson approved.

At about this time, and perhaps jokingly, Emberton remarked that his client had only commended the lighting of the building, and had never said anything about the building itself. Alec Simpson wrote:

> You mentioned . . . that while I had congratulated you on the lighting I had made no mention of the building. Firstly, the lighting is part of the building and not merely a feat of engineering, and I appreciate this very fully. Secondly, while I am very satisfied indeed with the way the building is going on I am - quite honestly - waiting for the jam at the bottom. But everybody I have spoken to think[s] that the building is looking just wonderful. At the moment I rather envy you. Your job will have been completed and your great satisfaction obtained by 29th April. But on that same day I start out on this great adventure. While I have neither lack of confidence nor enthusiasm I at the same time have a very full appreciation of the magnitude of the project and how much depends upon its success. Believe me, I am truly grateful for all the help that you have been and are being . . .

And three days later he wrote:

> I was at Piccadilly last night and the building seemed quite warm. The building is certainly growing on me - the more I look at it the more I like it.

In late March, one month before opening, Emberton's assistant, R H Pearson, took a telephone call from Stoke Newington. What was the biggest clear opening obtainable when the front doors of the store were open on Piccadilly? Pearson told the enquirer, who said that 'he was very doubtful as to whether this opening was large enough to get the aeroplanes in, which they intended to display on the fifth floor, and asked whether there was any other way to get them in.' Subsequently Alec Simpson rang. He would like to have the door posts removed to get the aircraft in, 'provided it does not affect the job architecturally . . . '

When the store opened, there were three aircraft on the fifth floor (for the first month). Associated with an exhibition on aviation prepared by Moholy-Nagy, they attracted huge attention and editorial space. Well, they would, wouldn't they. It is, as someone has commented, mind-boggling; and unfortunately no surviving files give any indication of precisely how this was achieved (presumably, by winching the aircraft, wings removed, up the staircase well) or how many people suffered nervous breakdowns in

Left: the facade and windows for the 'The British Season' in the eighties.

Aircraft on the fifth floor: in the foreground, the 'Flying Flea'.

Father and son . . .

styles and cloths to please them both

in the largest collection of ready-to-wear suits

ever carried by one store . . .

132 fittings   **6** GUINEAS
Second floor

SIMPSON 202 PICCADILLY (REGENT 2002) *have agents throughout the British Isles and will gladly send you the address of the one nearest you.*

Age a challenge, not a barrier 1937.

the process.

Alec Simpson had planned a great dinner at Grosvenor House to mark the store's opening. The guests would be his provincial 'partners in progress', and distinguished figures in politics, sport, and public life. At the end of March, inviting Emberton to the top table for the dinner, he noted that 'the acceptances so far are excellent indeed and I believe it will be the greatest gathering of the men's wear trade that has ever been.' A few days later he noted in a postscript to a business letter, 'Austin Reed has accepted our invitation!' He was understandably pleased and grateful that his father's rival was showing courtesy and kindness to a young challenger.

April 14: two weeks to opening. Alec Simpson wrote to Emberton: he understood that they were both in the store on most days, and sometimes missed each other by minutes. Why not synchronise? 'Any time after 9 o'clock would suit me, and if you would let me know your time, I will see that mine synchronises.' From that point, client and architect walked round the building together almost every evening, often guided by the Clerk of the Works, F C Lawrence, who had carried the stress of the day-to-day organisation of the building work.

April 16: Alec Simpson to Joseph Emberton.
    I wonder if you would do me a favour . . . In our bespoke tailoring department at the new store . . . I want to be at work on the day we open, and, in order that my cutters and tailors there shall be employed, I must get together from some of my friends 40 to 50 orders prior to the opening. We are employing only first-class Savile Row cutters, and our suits at 12 to 14 guineas are hand-made on the premises. We also do suits at 8 to 10 guineas, cut by the same men and made at Stoke Newington. Do you think you could favour me with an order, please?

April 17: Joseph Emberton to Alec Simpson.
    Dear Simpson - Thank you for your letter of 16th instant. I don't see that I shall be doing you a favour in buying a Simpson suit. It is a thing I have been looking forward to for a long time. All the sales talk about Savile Row cutters is unnecessary. I will make an appointment at once.

April 20 (less than 10 days to opening): Alec Simpson to Joseph Emberton:
    I went through the building yesterday evening and there appears to be such a lot still to be done. The finishing of the floors, odd bits of painting and decoration, carpets, furnishing, shop fitting and lighting, all seem to leave a lot to be done . . . I feel very much like the captain of a big new ship waiting for the pilot in charge of the tugs to get him out of dock, so that I can sail spick and span on my maiden voyage.

April 21
Traffic vibration cracked the newly-patented non-reflecting windows on the ground floor beside the main entrance in Piccadilly. The local authority required them to be made safe with brown paper, leaving the frontage looking frightful. The manufacturers promised replacements to be put in by Monday.

April 24: Alec Simpson to Joseph Emberton:
    After all the excitement on the 29th [the dinner at Grosvenor House] I would be very happy if you would call at my flat [near] Curzon Street . . . whenever the dinner is over.

On this letter Emberton has noted for his secretary:
    Thank him - say I shall be very glad to come along.

And so they approached the launching of Simpson Piccadilly.

THE THIRTIES

1936 Simpsons makes its first ever summer style statement: a double-breasted worsted suit with bloater and "whangee" cane; and hopsack Daks slacks with polo shirt and foulard square. Such fashion was to be timeless. Advertised in the popular papers it promoted a new leisure style for the younger smarter man.

The fashions are drawn by Hoff, one of his first for the firm. His relaxed square-jawed upstanding ideal men will be features of Simpson advertisements for the next thirty years.

WITH THOUGHTS OF SUMMER in mind, we offer you a few suggestions from Simpsons' vast array of appropriate clothes. The left-hand figure seems comfortable in a double-breasted suit—worn without waistcoat—at £6.12.6. The saw-edge straw hat and the whangee cane add a touch of seasonable light-heartedness. Right, the Daks trousers are in hopsack (30/-); the striped sports shirt (30/-) being neatly topped by a foulard scarf.

Simpson PICCADILLY

THE THIRTIES

Spring suits for 1936-7: the informal formal.
The clothes are bright and easy with broad shoulders and straight cut trousers. Available ready to wear and made to measure at £5 12s 6d for the flannel (l) and 8 guineas for the pin-head worsted (r) they are priced well above the high street outfitter but only a third of Saville Row charges with which cut and material stood comparison. The double-breasted suit is conservative high fashion and the light blue celebrates George VI's coronation year.

THE THIRTIES

The 1938 range straight to the retailer from the Simpson parent factory in Stoke Newington.
Fashion is moving. Shoulders are less stressed and jackets button higher. The essential overcoat was available single- and double-breasted and sporty and belted. Within the last sixty years, almost universal car ownership and central heating have made coats and hats obsolescent: concern for the environment may yet bring them back!

THE THIRTIES

1938 and fashion has loosened up since the mid 1930s: Jackets are shorter, lapels less featured and trousers wider.

(below): Padak raincoats were a Simpson speciality in the 1930s. (l-r) waterproof double-textured rubberised cotton; cotton gaberdine belted trench coat for town, a double-woven cotton slip-on.

(opposite): **Evening dress of 1936 in all its variants.** (l-r): full evening dress with tails; single-breasted dinner jacket in the forefront of US fashion with turn-down shirt collar and broad satin-faced lapels.
(below): "Tails slimmer waistcoat wider" in up-to-the-minute midnight blue, a colour only just popularised by Edward Prince of Wales. The white dinner jacket is a US innovation.

The 1936 Olympics made sports high fashion.

For the upmarket winter sports fan in 1937 there was skiwear, endorsed by Austrian champion Gerda Paumgarten; Swiss, Elvira Oströrig; German, Elvira Stürm. The styling is continental, the stay-up waistbands unassailably Simpsons. The suits, not cheap at 7 guineas, depend on quality tight-woven materials for wind and wet resistance.

Golf was the prestige suburban sport. Suede jacket, chamois waistcoat and lightweight Harris tweed plus-fours make a functional yet luxurious combination in 1936.

Block striped Crew Neck Shetland pullovers with plain coloured sleeves. (Navy, Black Green, Nigger.) 35/-

Ski or Skating Blouses.
A practical light-weight garment made of cotton and poplin, with ribbed wool neck and cuffs. Wind and snow proof. White only. Sizes 36"- 44" chest. £2.2.0

Ski-ing Suit
Heavy-weight Navy Gabardine. Fitted Blouse with elastic at sides. Pleated sides to jacket to allow action. Zip fronted, also pockets.

Navy Blue only.
Sizes 36"- 44" chest.
£7.7.0.

Bogey man

Two things strike us as pretty remarkable about the clothes being worn on the right. First of all there is the suit (represented here only by the plus-fours) which is made of the lightest Harris tweed we've ever set eyes on. It is especially recommended to you in blue (7 guineas) ... Then there is the suede jacket and chamois waistcoat—worn separately, or zippered together into one gale-defying whole. A really grand garment for 4½ guineas!

The cashmere pullover on left is a great deal of warmth for very little weight. 35/-. The alpaca one with collar is reversible, which is almost like getting two pullovers for the price of one! 70/-.

The stockings, believe it or not, are hand-knitted from Harris yarn. Price 8/6. The natural chamois gloves are reinforced with strips of hogskin, which give a magnificent grip. Their price is 12/6.

At no other time of year is the subject of golf shoes so topical. Both the above are pretty well swamp-proof and splendidly built. That on left, in best Scotch grain, costs 42/-. Right, in two tones of leather, 63/-.

© SIMPSON 202 PICCADILLY, REGENT 2002

3 THE STORE OPENS

O n the morning of Wednesday 29th April 1936 Sir Malcolm Campbell, the world landspeed record-holder, entered the store by the Jermyn Street entrance and walked through the ground floor to cut the tape across the front door in Piccadilly and declare Simpson Piccadilly open. It was open on that day to invited guests only: to distinguished figures from politics, the arts and sport, but particularly from the men's wear trade, and specially (in that group) Simpsons' 'customers' among the leading men's outfitters in the cities and towns of the provinces, and of London itself.

The note of innovation was struck immediately by the vivid colours and excitement of the window displays in Piccadilly and Jermyn Street. One

a

b

c

d

e

f

g

h

Opposite and previous page:
a Sports shop
b Ready to wear suits
c Dress and formal clothes
d Gift shop
e Barber's shop
f Sports wear
g Bespoke tailoring
h Outfitting.

1936: shopfittings and lighting by Joseph Emberton and merchandise display by László Moholy-Nagy.

was a 'sports' window, its width divided into three. To the left, five men's hats were placed above and around a dark trellis. In front were leant a dozen golf clubs, and six silver-topped walking sticks. Below the trellis were sports bags and a golf bag. The centre third (with a card of the store logo, fixed at an angle, with a golf club resting against it, the dark handle effectively 'pointing up' the name Simpson) featured five sports shirts fixed on a trellis in abstract shapes as if they were being worn, 'flying free'. In the foreground, four shirts were folded to body-shape, each with a tie knotted round the collar. The last third of the window showed four suits in different colours, the jackets on torso-stands raised on pedestals, the trousers draped below, with socks on leg mounts standing before them, and in the foreground, pairs of assorted sports shoes, neatly lined up. The display (by Moholy-Nagy) was effectively a still-life of men's fashion, including sports. It was like a stage-set, colourful and vigorous, and wholly new and original in the world of men's wear in 1936.

From the doorway, the visitor could see right through the store, from Piccadilly to Jermyn Street. Yet in the middle of the store there was daylight, achieved by the creation of a glass wall on the west side of the store, rising from the ground to the sixth floor, a height of 90 feet, half the height of Nelson's Column in Trafalgar Square. The great window embraced a fine staircase of cream Travertine marble, its handrail on one side of red lacquer on steel, and on the other of cream lacquer. The panels on the open side of the staircase were also of glass, allowing all possible light into the store.

Therefore the first impression gained was of spaciousness, light and colour. To the great surprise of the representatives of the men's wear trade,

The main staircase in glass and steel, 1936.

the sense of openness was emphasised in the display of stock: comparatively few items were on show in each area, and they were set out in a highly original way: shirts, for example, were shown on heat-formed plastic body-shaped stands. The majority of the stock was to be found in cupboards round the walls. These were of light woods, with contrasting paintwork in bright colours - red on some floors, and as background to the sports clothes and equipment on the third floor, sky blue and emerald green. The sales islands (which in many men's outfitters then were of glass, displaying the goods within) were also of veneered wood. Chairs were strategically placed for the use of customers. Some chairs were of modern bent plywood, others of chromed metal and red leather.

It was all uncompromisingly 'modern'; some called the style 'continental'. But the surprise of the representatives of the trade at these innovative settings were as nothing to their amazement when they began to examine the stock. First, they were astonished by the range of colours, at

Joseph Emberton's shopfittings. The tubular framed table was designed so that clothes could be displayed on the top, while the customer could hang his coat on the right-hand bar.

Stock cupboards with interior lighting.

a time when all professional men wore dark three-piece suits (with waistcoats), the majority in grey, black or dark blue, with white shirts and separate stiff collars. In the new store, most suits were two-piece, with the DAKS patented self-supporting trouser - the DAKS suit. And the range of colours and fabrics was beyond anything seen elsewhere.

Men's shirts, in 1936, were practically all tunic-style: that is, they had to be put on over the head since they did not open at the lower front. All the shirts in the new store were coat-style, as they are today. Shirts, in 1936, were almost invariably sold with separate collars (bone collar-studs at the back of the neck, hinged metal studs for the front). More than 70 per cent of the shirts in the new store were collar-attached.

Finally, a range of men's underwear was introduced. At this time, men usually wore woollen underwear, with buttons down the front and linen tapes tied round the waist. Alec Simpson had discovered in America a brand of cotton underwear, with elasticated waistbands and trim. Coopers' Y-fronts and vests were lightweight, body-fitting and cheaper than the older fashions. Few had been seen in Britain at that time. Alec Simpson, as was his custom when he was convinced that an innovation was right for

The Simpson gift shop, 1936.

An advertisement for the gift shop, 1936.

the trade, ordered a large quantity (the first samples were delivered across the Atlantic on the first scheduled commercial transatlantic flight, and arrived just in time for the store opening: the bulk of the order came later in enormous crates).

The merchandise policy could be summed up as quality and style with colours, and freedom and comfort in wear, irrespective of price, in both clothing and accessories: so trousers did not need braces, socks did not need suspenders, underwear trunks and vests did not need buttons, shirts did not need front or back studs (and did not have to be limited to plain or dull colours).

It was in truth a revolution; and as his distinguished guests and colleagues in the trade toured the new store, they were breathtaken by the audacity of it. Perhaps the lower ground floor caused the most comment, for the sheer variety of items on offer, many of them never before seen in a men's outfitters.

At the foot of the stairs, for example, was a dog shop, with several endearing Scotties. Other animals were installed - at least for the opening - including a marmoset monkey and a pair of Siamese cats. There was a tape machine (generally found in gentlemen's clubs, the tape machine rattled away giving the latest news and sports results, financial information and City prices). One could buy theatre tickets at a branch of Keith Prowse, travel tickets at Thomas Cook's, or make an appointment and leave messages for one's friends. There was a sports shop, a golf range, guns and fishing tackle, a gift shop for men and women, a flower shop, and a cigar, tobacco and cigarette shop (with cedarwood panelling that gave the area an inimitable aroma). The cigar shop was air conditioned, and an elderly Russian was employed to roll Balkan Sobranie cigarettes by hand. There was a barber's shop with 16 chairs, associated chiropodists and manicurists, and a 'shoe shine boy'. Men having their hair cut would be brought coffee by waiters from the restaurant. Also on the lower ground floor was a snack bar.

On the ground floor was general outfitting, a hat shop (with a range of round hatboxes floor to ceiling) and dressing gowns. The first floor

Shoe department (ground floor), showing one of the many rugs commissioned from contemporary artists, and laid on the cork floor. Against the shelving is a tall ladder for the use of agile staff.

The Simpson agents' clubroom on the fifth floor (subsequently the Simpson Services Club).

contained overcoats and raincoats, and the second floor DAKS suits. The third floor had tropical outfits, and sports clothes including riding kit. On the fourth floor was dress wear and other formal clothes, and - behind a glass screen - tailors were busily at work cutting and sewing: the bespoke service.

The fifth floor housed a great surprise: there were three aeroplanes. They were not very large: one, indeed, was known as the 'Flying Flea'. It is not certain whether a Supermarine seaplane was shown (it appeared in advertisements) but it was certainly to be seen in exhibition photographs, together with other famous aircraft of the time, such as the Gipsy Moth biplane. The aircraft were shown in a setting devised by Moholy-Nagy (no doubt associated with the exhibition he had mounted at the Science Museum the previous month for Imperial Airways), including photographs of famous aviators, and of the world's great airports. Of course the planes were a gimmick: there is no record that one was sold. But they made the headlines. (One journalist, no doubt writing from a press release without visiting the store, managed to report that 'Simpsons have an exhibition of moths on the fifth floor'.) For a few years afterwards, a rumour went round the West End that 'an aeroplane had landed on Simpson's roof'. There was plenty of available space then on the fifth floor, and the staff were encouraged to stay on after closing time on Fridays, to hold informal dances and play games - an extension of the Simpsonian Social Club which was a popular feature of the parent company at Stoke Newington.

There was another innovation on the fifth floor. The Jermyn Street end was closed off with a panelled wall. A central door led to a club-room for Simpson agents, as Alec Simpson had promised. There was a bar, and chairs and tables at which they could write letters or orders (for naturally there was a Simpson representative on hand to take orders). Outside the great window was a balcony, from which visitors could see one of the best views in London. Directly south is Westminster Abbey, Big Ben and the Houses of Parliament; St Paul's Cathedral and the City to the east; and the Surrey hills in the distance.

The opening day was a great success: yet the staff knew that it was something of a miracle that the store was ready at all. Two days earlier, on the Monday morning, 48 hours before opening, one of the young salesmen (the 16-year-old Bill Read) had walked into the store to find nothing in

The view south from the Jermyn Street balcony (probably taken during, or shortly after, the second world war; but certainly before the building of the Barbican and other post-war towers).

place, or so it seemed. In the middle of the ground floor a man standing on a soapbox like a policeman on point duty was directing the small army of staff as they climbed up from the basement with their arms full of clothing and accessories, to stock the cupboards and shelves. For no goods lift was yet running (the electricity supply had not yet been switched on), and everybody was working against time. At four o'clock in the morning the steps of the Piccadilly entrance were still littered with cement and rubble. As dawn broke, one of the young salesmen had his first haircut and shave 'on the house' in a barber's shop still being finished by the builders.

*   *   *

On the evening of 29th April 1936 Alexander Simpson hosted a grand dinner at Grosvenor House in Park Lane. Among the guests were distinguished figures in politics, the City, the press, and the men's wear trade. There were 600 people present. Many famous sportsmen were there: for example, one table included several Test cricketers: Percy Fender, captain of Surrey; R W V Robins, of Cambridge and Middlesex; Ian Peebles of Middlesex; and Percy Chapman, MCC captain on tours of Australia and South Africa.

But the trade support was what really mattered. The dinner was, as Alec Simpson had intended, the greatest assembly of his trade seen in his lifetime. The toast of 'Simpson Piccadilly' was proposed by Earl Winterton MP, and Lord Barnby. Replying, Alec Simpson particularly paid tribute to the work of Joseph Emberton, the architect. But he emphasised that the size of the building was less important to him than the quality of the goods.

Our especial pride is in the character of everything the store supplies. Though the tailoring departments alone cover 40,000 square feet, that is a fact of less importance in our estimation than the high quality of the clothes we supply. We are prouder, for instance, of the fine quality of our cigars than that the ground floor entrance has an unsupported span of over 60 feet, believed to be the largest in London.

The coloured floodlighting of the building will be one of the sights of London; but again that is only incidental to the main object of the store, which is to bring together in a convenient and pleasant setting all the best things that are made for men.

And what is all important to men throughout the British Isles and overseas is that we have hundreds of Simpson agents who can give that competent and complete personal service which is so much to be desired.

In making men more clothes-conscious and in raising the general standard of the quality of clothing for men, this new store should be of benefit to the whole of the textile industry.

Alec Simpson must have particularly valued the response to the toast of the Guests, for it came from Austin Reed, the founder of the now famous Store Group.

The opening of the store marks a new era in merchandising (he said). Many of us have been criticised in the retail trade for having had the temerity to purchase goods direct from the manufacturer. Today you have a

manufacturer of clothing who has opened in the West End a retail store with the object of making his merchandise known to the great body of potential customers in the United Kingdom, and you also have the sight of a number of retailers up and down the country welcoming this new step and cooperating with that manufacturer in his enterprise. I feel that Mr Alexander Simpson's enterprise is going to be tremendously helpful to all who desire to see the standard of clothing placed on a higher level.

The comments of the press reflected the general interest in the store, particularly its concentration on male fashions and accessories (Alec Simpson believed that it was essential to carry the men's outfitting trade with him at the outset: but there was already a strategic plan to introduce a floor of women's clothes before long, and this was in fact done within a year of opening).

The *Manchester Guardian* called Simpson Piccadilly: 'A bid to right the balance of sex equality - which we all know is now so heavily weighted in favour of women . . . Men, so rumour has it, dislike shopping . . . The aim of the founders of the new store . . . is to create an atmosphere where men shall feel at home, where they may buy not only their own shirts and socks, but purchase silk stockings for their womenfolk and presents for the family in a setting which is congenial and heartily male. Only the future can tell whether the attempt will succeed, or whether women will invade this new store in much the same way as they have monopolised all others.'

The Lady, not surprisingly, fought back: 'It is amusing to find that the man's shop is designed and set out with all the allure of one devoted to women's luxuries. Shopkeepers, evidently, do not share that masculine theory that a man always knows just what he wants and so is immune from display or advertisement.' *The Scotsman* called the new store 'an expression in every way of the modern spirit'. The leading trade journal, *Men's Wear*, gave three pages to Simpson Piccadilly, with the headlines:

Dogs, Aeroplanes, Flowers and Cigars Provide Quality Setting for Simpson Clothes

Colour, Glass and Modernist Simplicity Decorate Europe's Largest Men's Store.

Its summing-up reflected the ambivalent feelings in the trade about the new store. (There were plenty of people who gave it as their opinion that Alec Simpson, the youthful high-flyer, had gone too far this time.)

A true picture of a store and its possibilities can rarely be obtained from a visit before or at the opening. Give it a month or six weeks to settle down, and its competitors will know with just what or what not they really have to contend.

'Crazy' and 'magnificent' are two extreme adjectives that have been applied to this particular store during the past few months. We anticipate no narrowing of these extremes for some time to come; judgment pronounced following a mere visit must be based largely on personal taste.

Simpsons expect the store to be a profit-maker, of course. If it does not make a profit on its own account, they maintain that it will enhance the Simpson name to such a degree that. any way, it will increase considerably the business done on the wholesale side, and it is 'building for the future' all the time. Officially the store, as the largest Simpson agent, is, and will remain, subsidiary to the wholesale side - a very impressive subsidiary.

As the journal *Art and Industry* commented:

Hats off to Mr Alec Simpson for, whatever may be said about his store, it is a brave adventure.

Sorry I'm early—but look what I got at Simpsons!

Aeroplanes featured briefly in the Simpson range in 1936.

The 90-ft chromium light-fitting suspended down the main staircase well

The architectural press were almost unanimous in their praise of the new building, and it soon became recognised as Joseph Emberton's masterpiece. While the whole structure gives the impression of total simplicity, it is in fact innovative in many ways. Though steel framing for such buildings was not new, the design by the structural engineer Felix Samuely (another emigré) was novel : and after a long delay, during which several girders made by Dorman Long had been installed, the London County Council rejected the planning application, which had to be revised. This was no fault of Emberton or Samuely, but introduced further building delays. The architectural design of the frontage to Piccadilly was ingenious and complex. It looks austerely plain: but in fact, the white horizontal Portland stone strips are not vertical, as they seem at a first glance, but set at a slight angle so that they remain clean longer, and reflect the coloured neon lighting.

The interior also has many innovations. There are ducts ingeniously placed round the walls so that the lights hidden in them reflect off the ceiling: the front of these ducts are perforated with air-conditioning vents that are scarcely visible. Other suspended light fittings had electric bulbs shining not only downwards but also upwards, so that virtually no shadows were cast. Other ingenious fitments are never seen by the public. The water supply is by an artesian well housed in the basement, drawing up water from the London water table. There was, at the opening, an innovative vacuum system to clean the building, consisting of a vertical vacuum tube installed from basement to roof, with 'plug-in' cleaning tubes available on each floor, carrying dirt downwards (it was re-designed when the cleaners found the portable tubes too heavy). Yet another vacuum system was largely hidden in the ceiling ducts: this was the Lamson Paragon system for cash transactions. At each sales point, cash and invoices were folded into a cylinder which was placed into a vacuum tube, whisked up to the sixth floor, recorded by the cashiers and sent back down the tube with a receipt and change, a whoosh and a clank. It was a cumbersome system, and relied on accurate entries from the sales staff. In one house magazine the system complained in verse, beginning:

> My name is Lamson - you know me as Bill:
> A Paragon of virtue to salesmen, until
> They maltreat and misuse me, scribble and scrawl,
> And I'm no use to post-clerk or packer at all . . .

Computerised check-outs and the credit card have - alas for the romance of retailing - long since superseded this famous system, which was one of the few delights of small boys when towed along by their shopping mothers.

The character of the store is essentially the openness and spaciousness of each floor. In fact, each floor is divided into three sections, divided by steel fire doors. These are hidden behind floor-to-ceiling panels of mirror-glass, and are scarcely noticed by the shopper; but they can swiftly be put in place if it become necessary. The great central staircase provides the way out of the central section, and there are separate staircases, invisible to the public, at the Piccadilly and the Jermyn Street ends of each floor.

It is an extraordinarily ingenious building. The *Architectural Review* said of it:

> Mr Joseph Emberton . . . has set a standard of urban design that deserves emulation. Among the essays in various academic styles that form its immediate neighbours, his building stands out as noticeably sensible and

You can shave Blindfold with it...

PRESENTS THE

Packard Lektro Shaver

The first electric shaver sold in Britain was one of the novelties at Simpson Piccadilly.

contemporary, with real refinement of its own kind . . . A facing of Portland stone was demanded for this building by the landlords, but it has been used frankly as a facing material . . . The elevation is particularly effective at night . . . the modern demands of neon lighting having been fully recognised as an influence in elevational design. The interior has been very thoroughly detailed. The service demands of the different departments have been well utilised to give each its own character . . . while a homogeneity of style is preserved throughout the building.'

Later, that sharp critic of urban architecture Nikolaus Pevsner described it (in *The Buildings of England*):

Simpson's [is] an excellent, progressive piece of store design of 1935 . . . although it seems as first as if it consisted of nothing but the familiar bands of windows. However, the proportions, the placing of the name of the firm and the canopy of the top storey add just enough to show that here was an architect who handled the new idiom with conviction and personality.'

*   *   *

Once the store was open, the second wave of the launch strategy was started. This was the advertising campaign, planned by Alec Simpson and implemented by Bill Crawford and his agency, with Ashley Havinden responsible for the design and copy. It was a huge campaign, conducted in the newspapers and magazines (particularly those offering colour printing, such as *Punch*). In the first 15 months of the store's operation, £35,000 was spent on advertising (1990s values, about £900,000).

The flavour was set by whole-page ads in the London evening papers and the national mornings to coincide with the store's opening to the public on Thursday 30th April 1936. These announced the 'Opening of London's Men's Store', and cheekily purported to give 'Piccadilly traffic arrangements for today' - as if special arrangements were being made by the police. In those days, of course, all traffic in Piccadilly was two-way (not solely the buses, as in the 1990s). There was a bus-stop outside the front door and bus conductors soon got into the habit of calling out, 'Simpsons!' for the stop, which was valuable free advertising.

Most ads used one strong selling line - the first was: 'Look what I got at Simpsons!' and were illustrated by line drawings by the illustrator Frank Ford. In one, a young man is giving a Scottie dog to an older woman (she looking appropriately surprised): 'Sorry I'm late, but look what I got at Simpsons!' A man is giving a huge bouquet to a pretty girl: 'Sorry I'm late, but look . . . !' And for variety, a young man in flying helmet is climbing out of the cockpit of an aircraft, to the astonishment of a young couple: 'Sorry I'm early, but look . . . !'

Another ad illustrated a variety of country clothes and accessories, with cheerful copy: 'The various articles displayed for you on this page are taken, pretty well at random, from Simpsons' immense variety of clothes and odd things for the big outdoors. They are meant to illustrate two points. One, that though a man go tramping in the country there is no reason why the appropriate clothes should not be quite fun. And two, that there seems to be no end to the thoroughly sound ideas you will find in Simpsons.' A man is illustrated in DAKS, sports jacket and pork-pie hat and shooting stick, accompanied by a faithful Scottie. As usual when DAKS trousers were illustrated, there was the DAKS slogan that had become familiar in their advertising: 'One look tells you it's DAKS', in national newspapers also with the line: 'There is a Simpson agent in your district.'

The launching advertising campaign devised by Crawfords was immense. Scottie dogs may only have been in the store for a short time, but the illustrator Frank Ford made the most of them.

Sorry I'm late—but look what I got at Simpsons!

Race-going clothes were advertised for Ascot. Sports clothes were particularly advertised in (for example) *The Field*. Simpsons became a 'Sportsman's Paradise - for golf, tennis, fishing, cricket, flying, polo, squash, rugger, lacrosse, soccer, skating, shooting, hockey, darts, swimming, shove-ha'penny and indoor games'. At the end of June 1936 there was a chatty ad that exploited the current heatwave: 'This advertisement may lose something of its point if there's a snowstorm on the day it appears. But if the weather is as hot as it was when we wrote it, you'll be glad of the suggestions it contains . . .' These were, naturally, that one could buy lightweight suits, and summer socks and shoes at Simpsons.

The Gift Shop was doing good business. Ads suggested that *he* might buy *her* a handbag with matching belt, hand-painted metal flowers, a cigarette case, a bracelet, a powder box, a clip watch or a travel case. *She* might buy *him* Havana cigars, a Scottie, or a wine-bottle cradle in chromium plate.

Press advertising was accompanied by direct mail advertising by means of brochures designed by László Moholy-Nagy and Ashley Havinden, and printed in lively colours to make the most of the men's clothing stocked by Simpson Piccadilly. The wide range of colours in the suits, and the unprecedented colours of shirts (mostly collar-attached) for town wear as well as country, achieved a remarkable impact. Much of the impact was due to one artist, who had been discovered and brought to Britain by Alec Simpson. This was Max Hoff. Born and educated in Vienna, he was at this time 33; having studied portrait and landscape painting at the Vienna Academy, he had begun to make a name through his stage and costume illustrations. A number of his fashion designs had been published in the European journal *International Textiles*, where Alec Simpson saw them. He brought Hoff to London, and commissioned him to produce a series of illustrations of handsome, virile, sporting men - wearing Simpson clothes - that were to become the representation of Simpson style for a quarter of a century (joined, once Simpson Piccadilly added women's clothes to its stock, by fashionable, elegant and charming women). First used in the direct mail brochures, Hoff's illustrations soon became the mainstay of Simpson advertising. Bill Crawford recognised the power of this imagery, and when Hitler annexed Austria in 1938 Crawford persuaded Max Hoff to move to London, where he married and where his two children were born.

The store was certainly earning public attention and acclaim. In June, the members of the Design and Industries Association asked if they could make an evening visit; Alec Simpson personally gave them a guided tour.

Sales resulting from advertisements were closely monitored, and could be very satisfactory. A special promotion of DAKS suits resulted in 'greatly increased sales'; another for collar-attached shirts drew an 'excellent response, several dozen sold, and many direct enquiries'. During Wimbledon fortnight, an ad claiming that DAKS had been worn in every men's final during the previous three years, 'and by about 8 out of 10 first class players everywhere' drew strong sales of white DAKS.

By July, the aircraft had been moved out, and the ads advised a visit to 'The Boat Exhibition on the fifth floor. You will find there speedboats, outboards, sailing dinghies, collapsible boats and all manner of small crafts . . .' Another ad used the line: 'Down to the sea in slips!', illustrated by virile young men diving into the sea wearing Simpson bathing trunks. In the summer, a new line of cheaper trousers were added to the DAKS range – university flannels, Kantabs, priced at 21/-. In association with the American manufacturers, Simpsons promoted the Packard Lectro Shaver,

Max Hoff.

You hardly know you've got it on!

The Earl of Westmorland, who is known as one of the best-dressed men of our time, was so delighted with this coat that he allowed it to be called exclusively by his name

THE *Westmorland* OVERCOAT

Simpson PICCADILLY

Westmorland overcoat, 1936.

the first electric shaver to be sold in Britain, with the line: 'You can shave blindfold with it!'

As autumn arrived, a new lighter-weight overcoat was launched - the Westmorland, named after the Earl of Westmorland, 'who is known as one of the best-dressed man of our time [and] was so delighted with this coat that he kindly allowed us to name it after him.' (His autograph was sewn on to the label: he happened to be a friend of Lord Barnby.)

For the store's first Christmas there was a special air of activity and excitement, the ads inviting:

CHRISTMAS FUN AND GAMES AT SIMPSON PICCADILLY
Come and watch! Come and join in! Come and try your skill! Come and enjoy yourself!

As so often in the succeeding years, there was a sporting celebrity in the store to talk to the customers and advise them. In 1936, it was Peter Finnigan, the London and Home Counties darts champion. There were plenty of other attractions, including a model railway ('see the trains stop of their own accord when the signals are against them!'). There were conjurors, table tennis players, and many games to play - and to buy ('bring your friends, bring your family, and play yourself! Billiards! Devil among the tailors! Shoveha'penny! Darts! Pin tables! Poker dice! Scores of other games, old and new at Simpsons!'). There was even - a special novelty - television: on the fifth floor, for an hour each afternoon, John Logie Baird demonstrated his new development in home entertainment and information.

But behind the scenes, affairs were not so happy. The public were still flooding into the store, but the sales figures were not good. The store was certainly a showplace, but it was proving a very expensive drain on the resources of the parent company.

At this stage, the enterprise struck a rock. Simpsons' bank (Barclays) demanded immediate repayment of the overdraft (£200,000 - the equivalent of £5 million in 1990s values) that alone had made the store possible. The bank's argument was that the international political situation was unpredictable, and therefore the financial risk in financing a large new modern store was not one they could any longer carry (Hitler, having become Chancellor of Germany two years earlier, was beginning to threaten his European neighbours: Dollfus, the Chancellor of Austria, had been assassinated by Nazi stormtroopers in 1934). There are times when adventurous entrepreneurs need friends. Alec Simpson found such a friend in Lord Barnby, heir of a Bradford wool family, long a business associate of Alec and his father Simeon. He was a former MP for Bradford, President of the Confederation of British Industries, Past Master of the Worshipful Company of Woolmen, and a great figure in the City of London - a director of Lloyds Bank and the Commercial Union.

Lord Barnby speedily got to work, and enlisted the help of Edward Beddington-Behrens, a City financier who set up an arrangement whereby £200,000 was issued in Debentures and £200,000 in 5.5% Notes secured on the new building and guaranteed by the parent company, S Simpson Limited. This enabled the bank overdraft to be repaid, and in addition made available a further £200,000 to stock the store. From 2nd December, Simpson (Piccadilly) Limited was converted to a public company wholly owned by S Simpson Limited. Lord Barnby became a director of Simpson

THIS advertisement, as you may already have guessed, is about hats. It attempts the impossible task of giving you some idea of the variety of fashionable headgear to be found at Simpsons.

Starting, for want of a better place, at top left, you will see a black homburg. These hats (they are made in blue, too) are almost a uniform in London just now. Simpsons charge 27/- and 35/- for them.

Below that you may detect a trevor, with new-edge. Any occasion, this type may blaze up into furious popularity. For other 12/6 or 18/6 you can be trusty for it.

The hat below is almost as important to a fisherman as his rod and line. It is in Harris tweed, costs 1 guinea, and the first few come from our fishing tackle shop.

The polo cap, at bottom, is preferred to the helmet by most players today. This one costs 30/-.

Coming to the top again, you observe a tough flat-felt pork pie. Being a little narrower than usual. Narrow band, in cord or mohair. Choice of several good country colours. Price 1 guinea. The light grey suppers, which makes Ascot what it is, is London-made and costs 3 guineas.

Finally, there's the Simpson bowler - with its intelligent light contours weight, its rough hand-finish and its hand-tied bow - at 21/-.

SIMPSON 202 PICCADILLY, REGENT 2002

The Thatch hat 1936. For every occasion: (bottom to top) new style polo cap; tweed fishing hat; boater; bowler; top hat, grey for Ascot; Pork-pie; a novel navy blue Homburg. Hats were a fashionable essential but at 1-2 guineas not Simpson's cheapest accessories.

To mark the Coronation of King George VI and Queen Elizabeth in May 1937, the stonework of the Piccadilly facade was covered with trellis, carrying thousands of flowers.

(Piccadilly) Limited on 22nd December 1936.

Not much of this reached the press. The nationals had other matters to deal with that month. On 11th December King Edward VIII abdicated, and was succeeded by his younger brother the Duke of York, as King George VI. But as a result of these financial problems, Alec Simpson understandably began to question all expenditure, and to know when the bills would stop pouring in.

There were other problems at Simpson Piccadilly, involving the staff. Because of the financial difficulties, wages had to be cut. Alec Simpson decided that he needed one of his trusted lieutenants from Stoke Newington to sort out the conflicts in Piccadilly: he called into his office a young executive, Frederick Brame, and said: 'I want you to go to Piccadilly.' As 'Freddie' Brame told the story in later years, he said: 'But Mr Alec, I don't know the first thing about retailing.' Mr Alec replied: 'Well, now's the time to start learning.' In Brame's first week, one of the key managers resigned (the store manager, W P Yates, decided to return to the North) and soon afterwards Brame 'had to dispose of the services of two other senior managers'. Part of the problem - though eventually resolved - was that the staffing had been planned on a system that was then more usual in America than in Britain: the main staffing division was to be between merchandising (the buyers) and marketing (the salesmen and women). There was a strong system whereby each management reported to an executive, who reported to the board through the managing director. It was to prove effective (though not completely introduced in detail until 1950). Eventually, most promotions were made from within the store, and many employees, carefully chosen, stayed with Simpsons for virtually all their working lives. But at the beginning, as with so much else at Simpson Piccadilly, the system was novel and unfamiliar, and took time to be accepted.

For his part, Alec Simpson spent the Christmas holiday period reorganising the store. The flower shop, which from the early days had been losing heavily, had been closed. The dog shop, endearing though the Scotties may have been, closed in January. On 30th December Alec Simpson sent Joseph Emberton a five-page list of changes that were to be made by March. Most concerned the placing of more fittings, with more stock visible, particularly on the ground floor. (The winter had demonstrated that the main doorway open to Piccadilly let in a howling gale, and it was soon necessary to form a glazed lobby on the steps.) The number of chairs in the barber's shop was to be increased, so as to have 'at least one more chair than Austin Reed's'.

Preparations began for the Coronation of the new King and Queen, scheduled for 12th May 1937. Clearly this would be a great sales opportunity for the new store, since London would be full of foreign visitors from throughout the Empire. A new note of optimism began to spread through the business. Then on 22nd February 1937, Alec Simpson collapsed and was taken to the London Clinic. His illness was diagnosed as leukaemia, and on 15th May he died at his home, aged 34.

S Simpson Limited had truly been his life, and Simpson Piccadilly was his personal creation. Tributes to him from the trade were heartfelt: more than 2000 letters of condolence poured in. Some recalled his charitable work done as a vice-president of the Warehousemen Clerks and Drapers' Schools, and such charities as the Norwood Orphanage and the Bernhard Baron Settlement in the East End, where he had taught boys to box: he was a leader in the Association of Jewish Youth Clubs. He was a member of the Juvenile Advisory Committee, and initiated the Juvenile Employment Certificate for Stepney. He did not like these good works to be publicised, and preferred to be generous in secret.

At Simpson Piccadilly, one of the young assistants remembered the day, a few months earlier, when he was sitting at a table in the buying-room, working out a primitive stock control system. The door was flung open. There was the stocky figure of Mr Alec, who asked the lad: 'Who are you? What do you do?' He sat down, and said: 'And what ideas have you got for the store?' So the young man told him: and Mr Alec seemed interested, listening intently. Then he stood up, smiled and left. The lad realised that he had been talking to 'the boss' for half an hour, and Mr Alec seemed genuinely to value his opinion: never before having been a retailer, he made it his business to find out how every small cog in his machine was working.

*   *   *

When, nearly 30 years later (in July 1964), the French organisation Le Comité du Bon Gout Français awarded a gold vase, *La Coupe d'Or du Bon Gout Français,* to Simpson Piccadilly for 'good taste and elegance', Dr S Leonard Simpson accepted the award - given 'to encourage those organisations or personalities who work towards the betterment of international standards in fashion and gracious living, and who, by doing so, also contribute to their country's international prestige' - with the words:

> Any honour allocated for elegance and good taste must have a very special value if it comes from France, a country so sensitively and creatively attuned to these fine qualities . . .
>
> I would venture to regard this award as a tribute to my brother, the late Alexander Simpson, who not only founded Simpson Piccadilly in 1936 with courage and imagination, but who also laid down its sustained policy of quality, good taste and prestige.
>
> This policy has involved our continually searching the whole world for exciting and attractive merchandise on the one hand, and on the other sustaining and evoking the best traditional English clothing for men and women with beautiful fabrics, harmonious colours and modern graceful lines and innovations.

Alexander Simpson.

THE FORTIES

Fashion for the phoney war, 1939-40. This factory brochure still offers a pre-war range. For the older man a double-breasted suit, a conservative mid-1930s style; for the younger man a more boxey looser cut. Riding clothes and the blazer continue their traditional role.

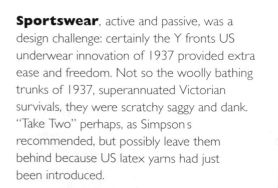

Wool — with front skirt 15/-

French model in heavy wool 25/-

'ool! 5 colours—white belt 17/6

Wool — Zip-fronted !

Sportswear, active and passive, was a design challenge: certainly the Y fronts US underwear innovation of 1937 provided extra ease and freedom. Not so the woolly bathing trunks of 1937, superannuated Victorian survivals, they were scratchy saggy and dank. "Take Two" perhaps, as Simpson s recommended, but possibly leave them behind because US latex yarns had just been introduced.

Easter notions

— a few highlights from Simpson's brilliant holiday display!

Sports and Country hats in finest fur felt 12/6 17/6 25/-

Sports and semi-hacking jackets of Saxony material in many new designs & shades 35/- 42/- & upwards

DAKS trousers 41 different colours 8 different materials 30/-

Brown grain Derby sports shoes, instep strap Royal and Ancient pattern sole 42/-

Heavy Scotch wool socks in many patterns and shades 4/6

Marcella shirts cut away collar attached 12/6 Twill foulard tie 4/6

Free Car Parking Facilities

Simpson PICCADILLY

Simpson 202 Piccadilly (Regent 2002)

Simpson PICCADILLY

Leisure and the long weekend were assumed for the new Simpson customer, though many new to prosperity after the slump must have found this detailed diagrammatic advertisement of 1938 as instructive as they were inspirational. The "Hacking jacket" was by now a general purpose sports coat. The more specialised "Shootin' and Fishin'" jacket, 1936, (below) was in traditional Norfolk style, functional with roomy pockets, a full cut back with half belt and vent. There are golf shoes with the leisure outfit and, beneath, sports and town shoes.

THE FORTIES

The Women's Floor, new in 1937, again targeted the weekend set with mix-and-match country tweeds in chocolate and green, lapels and pockets the only hints of high fashion; black sweaters, Vogue endorsed as snug warmth for cold country houses, depended on the client for the jewels; golf and shooting outfits, practical and adaptable.

THE FORTIES

Swimwear was stylish, one and two-piece wools as well as Lastex (bottom1) brand new from the USA. Equally novel were the continental beach shoes, raffia for men and wooden-soled for women. By 1939 Daks (bottom) had adopted the "3 piece suit' by adding a skirt to the matching slacks and jacket. Infinitely adaptable to work as well as play, it remained in the range through the austerity war-time forties. Tennis dress, 1939, endorsed by the champions, followed the functional man-tailored line.

What you need in an air raid

The Simpson tailored shelter suit—good looking and practical in every way. Slipped on as one garment in half a jiffy. Trousers detachable from the coat. In soft warm fleece — navy and natural. Price 70/- for men.
For women 69/6.
With a hood 82/6.

Peace or war? Simpson were equally prepared. In 1940 they stocked formal morning dress for the diplomat and shelter suits, for when all else had failed.

Here's a dress to give you a Spring feeling! Smart, superbly tailored, original just what you expect Simpson to find at Piccadilly! It's fine jersey, soft and comfortable. Colours are cherry, sky, oak, black, 7½ guineas

Wartime fashion in 1941; pre-war style in easy fit jersey but with the new shorter skirt. With 6 years of rationing ahead it was easily recycled into a pinafore skirt. Not many would buy them over the counter: they were the next season's sales bargains.

THE FORTIES

The 1940s "man-tailored" for war and pretty for peace.

The Daks suits (r) share the masculine, loose fitting square shouldered look, also adaptable to the ubiquitous 1945 "swagger coat". (bottom r) 1946, peace and naturalised French styling with curvaceous tight waisted jacket with flared peplum back. On coupons but not Utility, it also has a featured collar and a well cut pleated skirt. The blouse has become a Simpson staple. It variegated many a coupon restricted outfit. (top r) 1948 and peace brought multi-coloured Braemar twin-sets and American-inspired 'pedal pusher pants'.

Simpson PICCADILLY

THE FORTIES

Simpson
PICCADILLY

Simpson
TAILORED

THE FORTIES

Autumn 1948 and after a respectable 18 month delay Dior's extravagant New Look reaches Simpsons and austerity Britain. The elegantly conservative Frederick Starke model (r) was available in black, brown and grey with dull metal clasps. It was a pricey £17 6s 0d but only 7 coupons. By 1949, the curves had straightened to the "New Empire line", a town coat in French duvetyn. No coupons and available in pearl grey, olive green orchid pink and terracotta, Austerity was indeed at an end.

THE FORTIES

1947, 1948 (l-r) and at last the first peacetime flights to the sun, even if the equivalent of the restricted sterling travel allowance would hardly cover the cost of the colourful, extrovert US-inspired clothes. The shoes are 1946.

Ski-ing in style!

Back to the ski slopes: 1949, still in traditional style but soon to change as new synthetic yarns inspired the designers.

Simpson
PICCADILLY

4 TRADITION MAINTAINED

As was to be expected, Simpson Piccadilly did good business during the Coronation month of May. The stonework of the Piccadilly facade was covered with trellis from ground to roof, carrying thousands of roses. On 29th April, the store's first birthday, each salesman wore a carnation, each saleswoman a rose corsage, and a flower was given to each customer entering the store. In later years, the staff was served free food in their restaurant throughout the day, and at an evening reception in the store, a cake was cut and gold watches presented to staff who had served 25 years (later this became 21 years).

Obviously it would have been 'Mr Alec's' wish that the store should continue to uphold the best traditions of the House of Simpson. Mr Hollister, who had taken charge of the Stoke Newington factory during the chairman's illness, was made managing director of the parent company and also of Simpson (Piccadilly) Limited. In a statement, Hollister indicated that the businesses would be carried on without change, adding that in the 12 months following the opening of the store, turnover of the parent company had increased by over £100,000 (1990s values, £2.5 million). But one notable change, planned from the beginning, was implemented at Piccadilly shortly before the store's first anniversary at the end of April 1937: the fourth floor was transformed into a women's shop.

The first ads appeared in *Vogue* during April, promoting Knize suits for women. This was almost a transitional phase, since Knize 'of Paris and Vienna' was described as 'a man's tailor who also tailors for women'. At the beginning of June, however, there was a major newspaper campaign advertising 'the fourth floor: Simpson's Floor of Town and Country Clothes for Women'. The illustrations were of cashmere jumpers, cardigans, and Munro tweed skirts and hats. Later ads concentrated on what was called the 'Zipp! On dresses and gowns it has already become one of the joys of modern living. And now we have it on coats . . .'

Advertising copy continued to be witty. In the autumn, emphasis was placed on the sources of Simpsons' luxurious (and warm) fabrics.

FLEECE TO MEET YOU . . .

Three of our most valuable colleagues:

The *Bactrian camel*, besides possessing two humps and being pretty nimble on the feet, is very useful because of his long silky hair, which gives our camel coats their deep warm pile.

The luxurious fleece of the *Cashmere goat* has to be fetched all the way from Tibet. It's a long way to go wool-gathering, but this goat refuses to live in Europe. He's tried it.

The *Llama* lives mostly in the Andes, is a cousin-in-law to the Alpaca, and

The zip fastener promotion, 1937. Invented in the early 1920s, the zip first became fashion news in 1935.

Zipp!

ZIPP! On dresses, jumpers, and gowns it has already become one of the joys of modern living. And now we have it on coats. Beside the convenience of it, consider how well it looks. With a zipp a well-cut coat like this can reveal to-day's slim but curved figure at its best . . . . by eliminating the bulky wrap-over. Choose black and wear it in town with a bright scarf in the morning . . . . with your foxes in the afternoon.
7½ gns

Town and Country Clothes for Women, Fourth Floor.

FREE CAR PARKING FACILITIES

Simpson PICCADILLY

REGENT 2002

37/6
Daks only

The same outfit adaptable for peace and war.
Simpsons repeat the 1939 outfit in 1940, but the
price has risen just under 20%.

A model promotion 1937 featured Marcel
Rochas, a new innovative Paris couturier, if here
in rather muted mode, and Knize from Paris and
Vienna. Both models and copies were available
from Simpsons.

every year sends quantities of his soft strong hair which we blend so
successfully with merino wools.

'Women's DAKS - the perfect slacks' were introduced in the following year,
particularly aimed at women golfers. Another sporting promotion that
summer was a brochure associated with the Australian cricket tour. Most
of Alec Simpson's new introductions into British menswear, such as self-
supporting trousers, collar-attached shirts and 'American-style' underwear,
soon became the standard. The last were such a runaway success that
Simpsons started a wholesale distribution network through their provincial
agents, until eventually arrangements were made with Lyle & Scott of
Hawick to make them in the United Kingdom under licence.

In June 1937 Lord Barnby became chairman of Simpson (Piccadilly)
Limited, with H Hollister (of Stoke Newington) as managing director; two
other directors were Sir William Crawford (head of the advertising agency)
and Miss Lorna Tuck (the store's advertising manager). The company
secretary was Freddie Brame.

It was no fault of theirs that the results of the first 15 months of trading
(to 31st July 1937), published in November 1937, showed a trading loss of
just under £30,000 (1990s values, about three-quarters of a million
pounds). The trading loss for the following 12 months was reduced to
under £6,500 (about £170,000) - but this was before the payment of interest
on the debentures issued in 1936. The parent company nevertheless
welcomed this improvement, reminding shareholders that 'it was initially
contemplated that three years would be required to establish [Simpson
(Piccadilly)] on a profit earning business . . . it is gratifying to know that the
trading loss has fallen.' Indeed, in the year to mid-1939, the store showed a
trading profit for the first time.

*   *   *

So everything was continuing with some optimism, however long-term. But
for one man, the loss of Alexander Simpson was particularly challenging. His
elder brother, Dr Samuel Leonard Simpson, was at that time approaching
the peak of a distinguished medical career. At the age of 38 he had a practice
in Hampstead, and also a consultancy in Harley Street, where he was already
recognised as a leading figure in his speciality, endocrinology (the study of
glands). In 1938 he published a book, *Major Endocrine Disorders*, which over
the years remained in print as the standard reference work on the subject.
He thus had an extremely busy and demanding lifestyle. Now he was faced
with the challenge of what to do about his family firm. While he had been
very close to his father and his brother, and was aware of all major decisions
in the company, the demands on his professional time were extremely heavy.
In search of a second opinion, he went back to Cambridge and put the
problem to his old tutor at Downing College. Which life should he choose?
'You must do both,' said his tutor.

And so, astonishingly, he did (greatly sustained from 1940, when he
married, by his wife Heddy Monique, Baroness de Podmaniczky). He could
not, by the custom of the medical profession, direct a commercial business,
so Lord Barnby remained as chairman, and Dr Simpson ('Doctor', as he was
thereafter known to the whole company) became deputy chairman on 17th
November 1938. Sir William Crawford remained a director, and one more
director was appointed. The City was applied to for additional finance, and
Mr S H Gillett (a leading City accountant and 'company doctor', subsequently

TRADITION MAINTAINED 53

Sir Harold Gillett, Lord Mayor of London) was brought on to the board.

* * *

After a year of international uncertainty and difficulty, on 3rd September 1939 the Second World War broke out. Naturally, Simpson Piccadilly was prepared. As the ads (published from August) reminded the reader: 'A Commanding Officer forms his first impression from your uniform - Simpson's Uniform Department is on the first floor'. A week after war began, an Important Announcement from Simpson Piccadilly reminded the readers of the *Daily Telegraph*:

> Whether you are in H M Forces or on National duty . . . Wool pyjamas, waterproof trenchcoats, heavy aquatite shoes . . . Our Post Order Dept has been trebled in size. Our Civil and Military Tailoring Depts can fit you out at probably shorter notice than anyone in London.

The main men's ads in *Punch* rang the changes between young officers being measured for army or Royal Air Force service dress (a few months later, Simpson's dared to show a naval officer - daring, because one other London outfitter claimed almost a monopoly of Royal Navy tailoring). However, not even Simpsons could fit out all the services overnight; one new recruit noted at the end of September that his uniform hadn't arrived, and he had to man a gun emplacement wearing civilian dress - 'my brand new DAKS and my old Harris tweed jacket', for the use of which the army paid him sixpence a day.

Earlier in the year, the ads for the Women's Department had shown young women elegantly dressed in DAKS skirts, gardening trug on arm, doing a little light weeding. Now an ad appeared showing two young women in DAKS slacks and turbanned headscarves, one filling sandbags, and the other serving tea from a trolley. Later, a landgirl was shown, fork in hand, labouring with the Women's Land Army. (It was two years into the war before the ads introduced a young *woman* officer being measured for *her* service dress at Simpson Piccadilly . . .)

In part, the success of Simpsons in manufacturing and selling uniforms was due to Major Alfred Huskisson, who was appointed managing director of Simpson Piccadilly in April 1940. His knowledge of the menswear trade was considerable: he had been managing director of William Hollins of Nottingham (makers of Viyella) for most of the inter-war years. He was no longer young, but had a fine military record from the First World War in which he won a Military Cross and bar, and had excellent connections with the War Office. He had served in the Machine Gun Corps, and for many years the surviving officers held an annual reunion over dinner in the Simpson restaurant. A gregarious man, Major Huskisson was always impeccably dressed, with a carnation in his buttonhole. (When the popular television series *Are You Being Served?* was being shown, based by its authors on a fictional family retail store, Major Huskisson's carnation appeared in the buttonhole of the manager 'Captain Peacock', though the character was believed to be based on several Simpson staff of the day, notably Jack Wilson, then 'welcomer' on the ground floor. By sheer chance, one of the authors, Jeremy Lloyd, had worked at Simpson Piccadilly. So, as a youngster, did Christopher Lee, later a great film actor, who many years later recalled his happy times there, and the great impression made by 'Major' and his carnation.)

By this time the younger men among the Simpson staff were volunteering for the services. Soon the war came to London. The Stoke

Major Huskisson (left).

DAKS
TO THE
FORE

Slacks not slacking on the home front. Women's
sports and leisure trousers adapted easily to war
time workaday life. They were warm, functional
and valued stocking savers.

Newington factory was defended by a platoon of the Home Guard,
irreverently known as Dad's Army, since the majority of the volunteers
were men too old for more active service: not that they were inactive. One
of its members wrote an Ode in its praise, which includes the lines:

> They were all issued with some kit,
> Uniforms were made to fit,
> Battledress we're glad to learn,
> Were provided by the firm,
> Simpson's tailoring at its best
> (You choose the suit, we'll do the
> rest)!!
> To make the lads all nice and smart,
> The House of Simpson did its part,
> Caps alas were all too rare,
> Some their tin hats had to wear,
> Even these were not too free,
> They borrowed from the ARP.
> [ARP were Air Raid Precautions]
>
> On Simpsons' roof one dirty night,
> A Paratroop may heave in sight,
> To deal with him would be a trifle,
> If one only had a rifle!!

Despite these gallant preparations, on 18th and again on 20th September
1940 bombs dropped on north London, and the Simpson factory in Stoke
Newington was virtually destroyed by fire (the chief engineer, Frank
Marvell, was awarded the George Medal for bravery). Though the factory
was reopened with canvas walls, many of the 2,000 workers were no
longer in the neighbourhood, many men having joined the forces, and the
women having moved out of London. So additional factory space was
sought, first in Nottingham and then (in 1941) at Larkhall, near Glasgow.

The Piccadilly store remained open. It was fortunate that the structure
of the enterprise, essentially as a central supplier for a number of
provincial outfitters, meant that Simpson Piccadilly was entitled to claim to
be holding substantially larger stocks than other London stores without
such associations, and thus was entitled to larger allocations of the limited
quantities of civilian clothing manufactured during the war than would
otherwise have been the case. Purchase tax was introduced in 1940, and
clothes rationing began in June 1941, and remained in force until March
1949. The variety of cloth and styling was restricted from September 1941
by the introduction of standard 'Utility Clothing'. The staff worked long
hours; many - including the managing director, Major Huskisson, and the
company secretary, Frederick Brame - spending nights fire-watching on
the roof and balcony. (Freddie Brame was graded as unfit for military
service; the store was fortunate to continue to be served by his
undiminished energy: he was appointed a director of Simpson Piccadilly in
1944.) There were other wartime restrictions: to save power, and because
of the 'blackout', electricity could not be used for advertising (and the
famous light display on the Piccadilly frontage was turned off for the
duration). There were restrictions on the use of newsprint (since most was
imported across the Atlantic, and the shipping space was needed for food
supplies and munitions): the store's vigorous advertising campaigns were
cut back (and replaced by ads for a service repairing and restoring
clothes).

At the Services Club: Lady Louis Mountbatten in uniform.

The stability of the store's construction was proved when a bomb burnt out Lyons Popular Cafe on the corner of Church Place (and gutted St James's Church) but did only superficial damage to the store: the immense staircase window framed in cast concrete survived but with some of its glass broken. By 1940, the store had already begun what was to be a notable service to the war effort - the opening of the Simpson Services Club. The club-room already existed, on the fifth floor. It had been built into the original plans by Alec Simpson, as a club for Simpson agents when they were visiting London. It had comfortable sofas, chairs and tables for writing, a bar, telephones, facilities for a wash - and that magnificent view over London to the south. From June 1940, following the evacuation of British forces from northern Europe through Dunkirk, young men began to pass through London on their way to short leaves at home. Some would visit Simpson Piccadilly; and it was Dr Simpson who decided to open the Simpson Club to them. There the staff could telephone messages to their families, or find them a room to sleep, a bath, a change of clothing, a meal.

The Simpson Services Club remained open throughout the war. Membership was open to officers of both sexes. They merely had to be proposed and seconded; membership was free, and eventually there were some 12,000 members from all over the world. In November 1941 the first official luncheon of the Club was held, in honour of the Eagle Squadron - young Americans who had come to Britain to join the RAF (since America was not then in the war). The luncheon was attended by the American Ambassador, John Winant. Through the war, the Club hosted such events for the Canadians, Dutch, Australian, American, Belgian, Greek, Norwegian and Polish forces. One event honoured pilots of the Battle of Britain, many of whose dog-fights in the air over southern England had been watched from the Club's balcony.

In October 1959 the Duke of Edinburgh attended a reunion luncheon at the Simpson Services Club, at which Earl Mountbatten of Burma spoke of the generosity of thought which led to its formation, and to its value as a meeting place for service and ex-service personnel. He stressed its value during the war years as a place which 'enabled wartime leaders and officers to get together 'off parade' and, undoubtedly, many a point was settled in the Simpson Services Club which might not have been settled outside.' Lord Mountbatten was a regular customer, who always used to seek out his particular 'welcomer' on the ground floor, F J 'Bill' Read.

During the war, in addition to the use of the Simpson Services Club for social events, the Stage Door Canteen was opened in the BBC premises next door. It was on the ground floor (where the Joseph shop now is) with its entrance in Piccadilly. There many thousands of servicemen and women passing through London could relax, eat and drink. The 'canteen' was in fact a substantial theatre with a large stage, and patrons were entertained by the leading stars of London theatre, film and radio: Vera Lynn often broadcast from there. (In the late 1960s, linked to a small exhibition on the history of Piccadilly, a reception was held in the Board Room for founder-members of the Stage Door Canteen: the guests included Dorothy Dickson, Cicely Courtneige, Dorothy Hyson, Elsie Randolph, Wee Georgie Wood, Beatrice Lillie, Richard Hearne, Ruby Murray, Robertson Hare, Elizabeth Welch, Arthur Askey, Jess Conrad and Gary Miller.) The arts were also encouraged within the store itself: from 1942 responsibility for maintaining high standards of design and display was given to Natasha Kroll, a Berlin-trained designer who was delighted to find herself working

"I know a good uniform when I see one!"

This officer — a Major who went through the last War — was repeating a remark which is often made to us.

And it is not surprising.

When you have a firm as famous for its tailoring skill as Simpsons; when you realise that there are some hundreds of picked Service Outfitters up and down the land who are agents for Simpson uniforms and equipment — you see that this is indeed "the greatest Service link-up in the country."

Senior officers come to Simpson, Piccadilly, or our agents, because they know of our tailoring repute. Young men just commissioned come to Simpsons for their full outfitting and for expert advice as to what they need or don't need. . . .

In every town in Britain this organisation is at your service. (Army Uniforms — Tunic from 5 guineas and Trousers 2 guineas.)

Simpson PICCADILLY

UNIFORMS
AND EQUIPMENT

OVER 300 SIMPSON AGENTS, AND SIMPSON, PICCADILLY, LONDON, W.I

By September 1940, uniforms had become a principal feature of the store's trade – mainly aimed at men; but women officers were not overlooked.

He: "I like your uniform!"

She: "Simpsons, of course"

Trust a man to judge a uniform. By its differences, not by its likeness to his own. For him, precision. For you, precision cleverly combined with a flattering, moulded line. Simpsons tailor for both and they make the distinction very subtly. You can tell that at once by the set of the shoulders, the hang of the skirt, the smooth waistline.

Simpsons make uniforms for the W.R.N.S., the A.T.S., the W.A.A.F., and the other women's services. Agents all over the country have them ready-to-wear in sizes 12-32, and they take made-to-measure orders for quick delivery. Either way, you can be sure that your uniform will be perfectly cut and scrupulously correct in every detail.

Over 400 agents throughout the country, and Simpson Piccadilly London W.I

Simpson PICCADILLY

in an environment where she was given free rein, and generous support, to exercise her vivid imagination in creating exciting and topical window and store displays (she was later to be distinguished as a designer for BBC TV, a Royal Designer for Industry). Dr Simpson, himself a skilled artist, stimulated a series of exhibitions in the Piccadilly store. In 1943 there was an exhibition for Mrs Churchill's YWCA Wartime Fund; an exhibition of Brazilian architecture; another on Australia at War, and yet another on Aid to China. In April 1945, there was an Airport for London exhibition, and following the end of the war in Europe, an exhibition of Vampire jet plane engines.

On demobilisation after the war, each soldier was entitled to a civilian suit (known as a 'demob suit'), and S Simpson was among the tailoring companies commissioned to produce these in quantity. The code number for Simpson suits was Code 11; it is said that this fact was passed round the services by word of mouth at such speed that 'Code 11' suits went under the counter, and could only be obtained by asking the Quartermaster Sargeant very nicely. The production of these suits, following the great quantities of uniforms and battledress made during the war, meant that during wartime and its immediate aftermath S Simpson Limited had made seven million units of clothing for the Ministry of Supply for distribution to the services.

That Simpson Piccadilly was so welcoming a host to so many servicemen and women from around the world has resulted in a constant stream of visitors in the post-war years, returning to a London that had meant so much to them at a critical period in their lives. Many have brought their sons and daughters, and it is not unusual for tourists from abroad to visit Simpson Piccadilly because their parents had told them of its unique character - a reputation made in the hard days of war. Many famous wartime figures were customers. One salesman, Major A W Eden, having guided Field-Marshal Viscount Montgomery to the third floor to be fitted for a suit, suggested that 'Monty' might like to take the lift down to the ground floor. With his usual brisk manner, the great soldier remarked sharply, with a glance at the salesman's waist, that a little physical exertion incurred by walking down the stairs would do them *both* good. This was perhaps a little unfair on Major Eden, whose immaculate figure received customers at the front of the store with unruffled courtesy, treating new visitors with the same friendly welcome as the many famous faces from all walks of life, many of whom regarded him as a personal friend. It was Major Eden who, serving Field-Marshal Lord Slim, noticed that he was

The Simpson Services club in action.

(opposite top middle) A Piccadilly window created by Natasha Kroll to celebrate the liberation of Paris in August 1944, using the symbols of France - the tricolour, the Cross of Lorraine and the Marseillaise, with the winged Victory.

buying the cheapest gloves and suggested that he might like a better (and more expensive) pair: to which 'Bill' Slim replied, with a smile, that he had found that when making visits of inspection he often left his gloves behind, and therefore he deliberately bought the cheapest.

Gradually the staff who had volunteered for the services returned. Occasionally, as in many enterprises particularly in the much-bombed cities, there was some friction as those who had spent years at war in the Royal Navy, the Army and the Royal Air Force were told how those who had stayed at home had suffered the privations of rationing and fire-watching. The truth was that everyone had suffered, and all were weary. There had been hopes that at the end of the war, life would become easier. Sometimes in the years after 1945 it seemed that life was becoming much more difficult. The Labour government elected in that year battled to introduce social improvements planned and promised during the war - nationalisation, the national health service - but they were faced with shortages of materials, and an economy critically weakened by war.

By the end of 1947, the workforce of the store reached 500 (at the opening, a decade earlier, there were 300). Major (as Huskisson, the managing director, was known throughout the store) had circulated a monthly bulletin to keep the staff informed of developments. With the increase in staff, he introduced a 'house magazine' which he named *Trend*. At first it consisted of only a few pages. In its first issue (February 1947) there was good news and bad news: the good was that the manufacture of DAKS, discontinued during the war, was being started again, and customers could be told that the store's great selling line would be available later in the year. The bad news was that the Board of Trade had issued regulations limiting the permitted retail mark-up on clothing. However, despite fuel restrictions that limited heating and lighting, so that for some days the store was largely lit by candles and the staff wore overcoats and scarves with temperatures near zero, the spring sales turnover was up on the previous year. (The parent factory at Stoke Newington continued to manufacture in this period – despite the loss of its mains electricity supply - by hiring a fairground generator that was discovered nearby, in store for the winter.)

In March the Sports Equipment department was opened on the first floor, with a Sports Centre opened by Lord Aberdare in the presence of three leading cricketers (Sir Pelham 'Plum' Warner, R W V Robins, and Jack Hobbs) and leading figures from the worlds of golf, tennis, table tennis, squash, skating, billiards, athletics, football and rugby. There were even golf nets, with Willie Ritchie (a noted teaching professional) available to give advice. In July Australian cricketers visited the store, and Sidney Barnes mentioned that when the MCC had been touring in Australia during the winter, both teams had been wearing DAKS. It was an acknowledgement of what was to become the custom for many years: Simpsons would kit out English teams with DAKS trousers and blazers, and invite the leading visiting teams to a reception in the store, presenting them with two pairs of white DAKS each. (The same links were soon established with other sports, notably golf, tennis, and winter sports). In 1948 the Australian team captained by Don Bradman won the Test (and Barnes, Lindwall and Hassett celebrated by visiting the store to buy Simpson suits). The West Indies touring team were kitted out at Simpson Piccadilly. In 1949 the New Zealand team was welcomed to the store, and a cricket reception was attended by Jack Hobbs, 'Wally' Hammond and the

Queuing for DAKS, when they arrived back in stock after the war. The queue stretches down Piccadilly past St James's church.

Bedser twins. That year also, the Combined Universities Athletic Team attended a reception, preceding their American tour, led by their captain 'the new athletic star' Roger Bannister (who in 1954 ran the first four-minute mile at Oxford). That reception was held in a store exhibition titled Foot Comfort in Action, and including Queen Victoria's and Prince Albert's skating boots, Gordon Richards's riding boots, Bill Edrich's cricket boots, and stage boots worn by Dolores Gray.

By the late 1940s DAKS were being made once more, and the store was receiving supplies from time to time. When rumour spread through the West End that a new consignment had arrived, a queue would form in Piccadilly. As the queuers entered the store, the salesmen would go down the line measuring inside leg and waistband, so that when the eager purchaser reached the sales point, a pair of precisely the right size would be offered to him, sometimes with a choice between two colours. DAKS suits were also coming back, and for the first time, in response to an international trend, a lightweight version was added to the range. But sometimes the customer did not understand the particular qualities of DAKS. A legendary story tells how one such customer, having bought a pair of trousers, asked that buttons should be sewn on the waistband for his braces. When the heresy of this was pointed out to him, he said that he always wore braces. Since the customer is always right, he was politely directed to the Gift Shop, where clip-on braces could be bought.

It was another customer who, during a special promotion for the Simpson trilby hat (marketed under the trade name 'Thatch') approached a salesman and asked whether it was true that they were made of rabbit fur. Yes, he was told, as well as other furs such as beaver, nutria and silver muskrat. The customer thought deeply. 'Tell me,' he said, 'how do you manage to breed them in all these different colours?'

Meanwhile, in answer to calls from the government that British industry must rebuild the country's economy by concentrating on exporting to earn foreign currency, and particularly American dollars, the parent company was developing an export trade. In 1948 Major Huskisson (as joint managing director of S Simpson) led a coast-to-coast export drive, holding promotions for the representatives of the leading men's wear stores in

America and Canada. He was accompanied by the store's display manager, Natasha Kroll, whose job while in Los Angeles included 'casting' a procession of young Hollywood extras for their 'British' looks, and thus as suitable to model DAKS. In 1948 the store played host to a great many overseas visitors, and particularly the leading sportsmen and women, since the first postwar Olympic Games were held at Wembley, and many international athletes were welcomed to Piccadilly.

As part of the export drive, an Information Bureau for overseas visitors was opened, giving information on purchase tax, export licences, and methods of payment. Within two years, a full Export Department had been created on the fifth floor, designed by Natasha Kroll and built (in record time) by the maintenance staff led by Fred Clenshaw, and soon providing one-eighth of turnover. To make space in the store for the new Export Department, the workroom (making alterations to off-the-peg clothing) was moved out to rooms in Lexington Street, nearby in Soho. The bespoke tailoring department, where customers could watch suits being hand-crafted - one of Alec Simpson's original ideas, remained in the store until 1960.

Gradually the country's economic state began to improve, and in mid-March 1949 clothes rationing was ended and the dreaded 'coupons' - which had to be given up at the time of purchase - were discarded. In one of the Piccadilly windows (the curved non-reflecting glass had just been restored) was placed a large wastepaper basket, overflowing with clothes coupons and bearing the legend: 'Stop Press! All clothes are off coupons!' One salesman remembered how, the year before, he had said to a pleasant lady customer how nice it would be when one could buy clothes without coupons: she whispered to him, out of earshot of other customers, that she thoroughly agreed, but she was Lady Cripps and her husband Sir Stafford (then President of the Board of Trade) was responsible for 'those awful coupons'.

Despite difficulties of supply, Simpson Piccadilly did its best to demonstrate its pre-eminence in fashion. Evelyn Whiteside, as manager of the women's shop, visited the Paris collections (noting in 1947 that 'all suits have longer jackets and very slim fitting skirts, or the other extreme - skirts with large box pleats all the way round', while 'sweaters were long, in the American Sloppy Joe style, in colours of greige (grey/beige), mushroom, banana, lilac or Navy blue'). Miss Whiteside also instituted a series of evening private views of the Simpson collection: her effectiveness as buying executive in these difficult years enabled Simpson Piccadilly greatly to raise its stature in the women's fashion trade in the west end. To strengthen the store's reputation in women's fashion, Doctor Simpson persuaded his wife to accept appointment as a director, and Mrs Heddy Simpson attended her first board meeting in May.

From this period, Simpson staff were often sent to major sporting and social events to keep abreast of international fashion. These included not only the Paris collections, but ski centres in Switzerland and Austria, French Riviera summer resorts, and the major British fashionable sporting venues such as Ascot, Goodwood, Wimbledon and Henley. Staff were also sent regularly to visit the store's major suppliers, to see how garments were made. Cashmere was becoming a major success, particularly in the American market, and a Simpson visitor to the Scotland Mill of Pringle & Co. at Hawick in the Scottish Lowlands noted that 'by far the biggest percentage of yarn used is pure Chinese Cashmere from the fine down

Within hours of the ending of clothes rationing in March 1949, one of the Piccadilly windows announced the news - with a waste-paper basket stuffed with the hated coupons.

Lord Barnby, left.

fleece of the Cashmere goat found in Northern China and Tibet . . . Other rare fibres like super angora, alpaca, lambswool and Shetlands are included in the Pringle ranges.' Simpson staff regularly visited the leading names, such as Ballantyne of Innerliethen and McGeorge of Dumfries. There was to be a special promotion at Bonwit-Teller, the leading store in New York's Fifth Avenue, showing Cashmere sweaters in eight pastel shades with lightweight skirts in the same shades by Wilson & Glenny, also of Hawick. Another Simpson visit to Hawick was to Lyle & Scott, who at the instigation of Alec Simpson at the opening of the store had made a great success manufacturing American-designed Y-front underwear. Naturally, there were also regular visits to William Hollins Limited of Nottingham (of which Major Huskisson had been managing director between the wars), manufacturers of a staple of Simpson Piccadilly - the Viyella shirt (the name was derived from a Roman road, the Via Gellia, at Cromford in Derbyshire, whose spinning mill became known locally as the 'Vi-Jella' mill, and then 'Vi-yella').

By 1950 the house magazine was remarking that 'a noticeable informality and casualness has crept into men's town and evening clothes', and since Simpson Piccadilly had been designed by Alec Simpson to reflect precisely such a liberation of colour and style in men's clothing, the store was excellently placed to make the most of this change. Indeed, when in the following year London attracted numbers of visitors to the Festival of Britain, the postwar celebration and funfair on the South Bank, Simpson Piccadilly became something of an extension of the Festival. The fashions of the Festival - natural woods, plastics, metal furniture, clear graphics - required the store to do very little updating from the characteristic forward-looking style established at the store's opening, 15 years and one war earlier.

It was a busy period. The demands on the staff were considerable. But Major Huskisson and Freddie Brame, supported by Lord Barnby as chairman and Dr Simpson as deputy chairman, had made a particular effort to ensure that the work of the staff was recognised and acknowledged. Each year in the approach to Christmas, 'Major's Party' was held in the store, at which - for a number of years - Major Huskisson and the directors entertained the staff, and were entertained by them (from 1947 it was the custom for a concert-party to put on a musical revue, for many years led by the general manager Reggie Cross and his wife - he the author of witty verses on store affairs, she a skilled pianist and accompanist, enlisting the help of other staff members who often revealed surprising talents). For their part, the staff of the store invariably presented Major each year with a new pair of pipes (while wondering what he did with so many: one year someone asked him, and he replied that he smoked them). It was a busy period, for in the week before Christmas there was invariably also a party for the children of staff, who were invited (by the Major) to perform their party-pieces. The climax, naturally, was the arrival of Father Christmas (for many years looking surprisingly like the genial and kindly Bill Millard, for many years Simpsons' 'welcomer' at the Piccadilly entrance).

In Festival year a new Tropical Department was introduced. Sales staff were instructed on the characteristics of new man-made materials. For example, was Nylon suitable for tropical wear? Nylon, it was reported, was mothproof, but 'is it equally proof against silver fish?' The answer: 'Silver fish do not feed on Nylon, but if they are trapped in a Nylon fabric they will attempt to bite their way out, and thus may cause damage.' In 1951 there

[From TREND 1955] Christmas 1955 - and the store becomes the home of a cigar-smoking Father Christmas – by the great French illustrator André François.

A buffet in the Madison Bar, 1954;

Christmas present display, 1954

Gifts for Her, Christmas 1956.

was a Cricket Week, with Denis Compton and Godfrey Evans as the stars. Sadly, the manager of the Sports Centre, Ronnie Curson, died that summer aged 48: he was much missed; his colleagues remembered his skill at tennis, cricket, golf and skiing, and the sports stars - Gardner Mulloy, Budge Patty, Jaroslav Drobny, Louise Brough and Frank Sedgman - who had looked on him as a friend. He was succeeded by John Palmer, a good friend of Fred Perry, Jack Kramer, Lew Hoad, Ken Rosewall and later Panchos Segura and Gonzales. Since in those days play at Wimbledon was only in the afternoons, the tennis stars used the store and its Club Room as their base in London. Indeed, Jack Kramer once scandalised a BBC interviewer at Heathrow Airport (in the days before advertising on TV) by answering, when asked what he was going to do first in London: 'I'm going to see my friend John Palmer at Simpsons in Piccadilly.' (John Palmer also distinguished himself, working closely with Natasha Kroll, as advertising and promotions manager.) The refurbished restaurant was launched with a party attended by Jimmy Edwards, Joy Nicholls and Dick Bentley, Arthur Askey, Alistair Sim, Geraldo, Mr and Mrs Leslie Henson and Brian Reece.

The best graphic artists were used for Simpson advertising, led by the inimitable line of Max Hoff, whose elegant men in City (DAKS) suits or country (DAKS) trousers and tweed sports coats, accompanied by women of fashionable elegance (often in DAKS skirts and cashmeres) came to epitomise Simpson style in national press advertisements. Visiting Paris, Natasha Kroll recruited the distinguished French illustrator André François, who designed a memorable Christmas display including a cheerful cigar-smoking Father Christmas and some wicked young 'angels': he also designed menu cards for the restaurant, and a set of Simpson playing cards. Miss Kroll kept an eye open for promising young designers: one who had his first display furnishings shown at Simpsons, when he was just out of art school, was Terence Conran. Natasha Kroll designed a graphic presentation for the new Madison Bar, involving the typography of the word Madison turned sideways to form a skyscraper: it was only one symptom of the growing volume of DAKS exports to the United States and Canada, attracting more and more American visitors to Piccadilly. Another American touch was the use in advertising of the witty drawings of Alajalov, famous for his covers for the *New Yorker*. One Simpson Christmas poster was by F H K Henrion FSIA. All this advertising was placed through the Crawford agency, where Bill Crawford aided by Ashley Havinden had done so much to establish and maintain a strong public image for the store

a

b

c

d

a The Woman's Department, 1957 with a rug made economically from carpet samples supplied by the trade;

b Evening wear in a theatrical setting, 1956;

c The Young & Gay Department, 1962;

d A window for the Motor Show, 1953;

e A window for Ascot, 1953;

f Christmas in the Woman's Department, 1960;

g André François window, Christmas 1955 (right).

since its opening. Sir William Crawford - Alec Simpson's adviser and friend from the early days, subsequently a director of Simpson Piccadilly, and a powerful influence on the development of the store - died in November 1950, just before government restrictions on the use of print, paper and advertising were lifted and it became possible to produce still more vivid and imaginative literature and promotional material.

A lavishly illustrated and colourful brochure was produced for Festival year, and 6,000 copies were distributed to overseas travel agents. It began with a romantic meeting with the statue of Eros.

So dreamlike was the air of the amber-coloured afternoon that the little knot of London's guests were scarcely surprised when the god Eros addressed them from his pedestal in Piccadilly Circus.

e

f

'I am an immortal,' he began in English, for his native language, ancient Greek, would not have been very helpful. 'Perhaps I need scarcely mention it, for no mortal could have survived sixty winters in my present costume. To humans,dress is more important. Indeed, ladies, I understand, sometimes count it more important than food. In London, as no one denies, the finest men's clothes in the world are found, and for women's clothes of certain types these islands have never been equalled.

'For both sexes this is a propitious spot. Not a bowshot from here is a store unsurpassed anywhere in the world. But especially rich in those very goods for which Britain is most famous. And thoughtfully organized to assist the guest from overseas. Let me show you. And also give you some information which will make it easier for you to find London's most

The Festival of Britain had a strong impact on display in the early 1950s: here a show of shirts, ties and socks is created from the spindly metal, and wood or plastic ball-feet typical of the period (an early work by the young design assistant Terence Conran).

attractive places of interest and entertainment.'

So saying, the god sprang to the ground in a decidedly immortal manner and led his followers a few yards down Piccadilly to Simpsons' unmistakeable building . . .

Now walk round and see for yourself the wealth of good things for men and women who understand the art of dressing well. And the many ways in which Simpsons is eager to serve you. A particularly warm welcome awaits the visitor from overseas.

In the following year, Eros was joined in the promotional brochure by the goddess Diana (hunting good clothes, naturally).

'The rumour has reached Olympus,' she said 'that Simpson of Piccadilly is a happy hunting ground for the woman who likes smart clothes with a sporting flavour.'

'That's perfectly correct,' responded Eros. 'Many's the time I've directed a mortal there. She has gone in human and emerged looking divine.'

The year 1952 began with the death of the King, George VI, and the accession of his elder daughter as Queen Elizabeth II. The new reign heralded a period of optimism, and this was reflected in the increased variety of goods that were being produced in Britain, and offered for sale in the best stores of the West End, such as Simpson Piccadilly. Yet more novel fabrics were being created (salesmen were told about 'a British synthetic fibre, Terylene, produced here in small quantities by the ICI'). But the staple of Simpson garments remained wool: the International Wool Secretariat sponsored a Wool Fashion Week in the store.

g

DAKS were now available in 14 different materials, with 49 patterns and colours (one had been designed at the Stoke Newington factory: 'Balton' cloth, named after Henry Balcon and Bill Preston of the parent company, and woven at Salts (Saltaire) Mill outside Bradford). The characteristics of DAKS worsted flannel cloth were described for the information of Simpson salesmen, to pass on to customers:

Many sports trousers are made from 'piece dyed worsted', that is to say, the cloth is woven from white yarn and dyed after weaving. Standard DAKS numbers, however, are what is known as 'wool dyed'. The wool is dyed in the raw material state and blended to the required colour, and actually woven in the coloured state. It is interesting to note, for example, that the lovat shade, 611, contains no fewer than 11 different shades. A point of interest to both the salesman and the customer is that a cloth of this character will wear for a much longer period than will a piece dye without becoming shiny.

The wool which is used in the manufacture of DAKS cloth is pure merino. This, in its raw state, passes through a process which is known as the 'combing operation' and has the effect of ensuring that the wool fibres run parallel, enabling a fine yarn to be spun. This yarn which is of great tensile strength when woven, is capable of standing up to the strain of everyday wear, while at the same time retaining the splendid appearance of the cloth.

The strands of yarn are twisted together, and it is this two-fold thread which, woven into the DAKS worsted flannel cloth, gives it the strength and durability for which DAKS trousers are now so famous.

During the 1950s Simpson Piccadilly played host to a wide variety of exhibitions and displays, some not necessarily associated with clothing, but with national or London associations: the first exhibition of the decade, for example, was 'Inside Scotland Yard', and was opened by the Commissioner of the Metropolitan Police, Sir Harold Scott.

But many of the special events were linked to sport. In 1950 Dr Simpson initiated the £2,000 DAKS Golf Tournament, played that year at the Royal Mid-Surrey. It immediately took its place as an important event in the sporting calendar, was accepted by the Professional Golfers' Association, and became the first professional golf tournament in Britain to be televised by the BBC (then the sole television provider). Dr Simpson was himself an enthusiastic golfer, as his brother Alec had been; and indeed DAKS owed their creation to Alec's determination to introduce more comfortable

1950: the Hat Department made a wall feature of hat boxes.

The Sports Department, 1950.

Continued on page 75

THE FIFTIES

By 1956 for ski wear Lapland-type parkas combine with
sleek flexible fit lycra-mix pants.

Home and Away, Simpson man has never had it so good as in the mid 1950s. In the country, 1955, he relaxes in almost pre-war comfort in sporty tweeds, while for tennis and golf there are the Daks shorts and slacks, easy fit with self-supporting waistbands as well as the zip-front cardigan, which will remain in the wardrobe, moth permitting, for the next forty-five years. By 1957 (opposite) style has become international. The slightly more fitted suits with their long lapels blend US easy styling with a slightly more fitted Italian line. And, on the beach, 1957, there is transatlantic comfort in colourful denim and cotton knits.

Golf Monthly (2 colours) March

It's a matter of course...

... go to all Simpson tennis clothes for their comfort-on-court and their cool good looks at the stickiest point of the game. These famous Daks tennis shorts are beautifully cut, and have concealed pads in the waistband to control the shirt. In white worsted, or in the finest wool gabardine, £5.10.0. Also this luxurious heavy-knit pure-wool cardigan. Splendid for cooling down after the game. It has a zip front and raglan sleeves. 8 guineas.

for most keen golfers to tee-off each season with a visit to Simpsons, in Piccadilly. For here they take a professional, links-eye view of golfing matters. The result: the warmth and freedom of movement of this heavy-knit golfing cardigan. It has a zip front and raglan sleeves. In black, maroon, bottle, natural, and white. 8 guineas. And: the firm footing provided by these Simpson 'Sura-tees' golf shoes. This latest lightweight style is in supple brown calf with moulded rubber sole. 5 guineas. Also in two-tone brown/white or black/white with rubber soles, 5 guineas.

Visit the Tennis Shop on the first floor.

Simpson (Piccadilly) Ltd, London W.1 Regent 2002

Simpson (Piccadilly) Ltd, London W.1 Regent 2002

... right round the world

Shore lines...

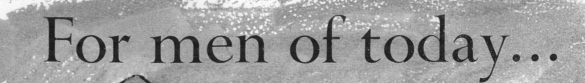

Punch, April 8 1959

For men of today...

it's

a

DAKS

world !

Simpson
TAILORED

In the "World" promotions of 1959-60 Hoff
illustrates the three fashion trends (l-r) the Italian look, Brioni
inspired, with short high button jacket; the retro Edwardian
look, guards officer based, and complete with bowler hat; the
looser transatlantic cut with the long low shawl collar on the
DJ. And, of course, the omnipresent accessory – woman!

THE FIFTIES

THE FIFTIES

Woman goes straight; the slim fitting suit of the early 1950s soon succeeded the exuberant New Look, though this was still available to the nostalgic Simpson customer in 1950 (bottom l). More fashionable perhaps was the swing-back coat (l-r, 1953, 1950, 1950, 1952).

First class for travel anywhere. Our big casual coat of vivid checked 'Otterburn' tweed. The view from the front — wide notched revers, three leather buttons in a row, two tabbed pockets. Hip sizes 36-41, in these three brilliant colour ways. The price, 16 gns.

A *Dellburg*

MODEL

FROM

Simpson PICCADILLY

New high-style British fabrics gave home grown fashion a new image in the 1950s. (l-r) a tweed top coat, 1953; a "stem-slim" Daks skirt with a "never slip waistband", 1958. From the Simpson Jubilee catalogue, 1957: Fredericka cottons including an up-to-the-minute short evening dress; up-market Mods with the essential Lambretta, as well as twin set and tweeds.

THE FIFTIES

For the new world wide leisure market of the 1950s there was the "Daks trio", their linen capsule holiday wardrobe of 1958 which includes play shorts with optional wrap-around skirt as well as "slinkies", the slim fitting trousers which were replacing the traditional Daks slacks as illustrated in 1951. New elasticated materials were to make easy fit less a matter of cut. Retained was the wide Daks choice: 11 colours and 5 materials for the trousers and 15 colours for the Trio.

To mark the Simpson winter sports reception in 1952, Austrian woman ski champion Erika Mahringer gives some tips to young actor Richard Attenborough in rehearsal for his new play *The Mousetrap*.

HRH The Duke of Edinburgh welcomed by Major Alfred Huskisson on to the DAKS stand at a trade fair.

Continued from page 64

Simpson considered it only fair to sponsor a Ladies' National DAKS Golf Tournament, and this was held for the first time at Wentworth in 1954. It became customary to hold receptions in the store during these tournaments.

In 1951, during the Festival of Britain, the store mounted a display of British racing cars. In the tradition of achieving the near-impossible, introduced by the display of aircraft at the opening of Simpson Piccadilly, five racing cars were manhandled up to the third floor, and a further three, including the green ERA (English Racing Association) car, and the record-breaking Cooper Mk.5, were shown on the ground floor. The exhibition was opened by the veteran British racing driver, Lord Howe.

Every year there was a special promotion to celebrate winter sports, and especially ski-wear, marked by receptions in the Store, and the presence of European ski champions to give informal advice for two or three weeks (in 1952, the visiting expert was the Austrian champion Erike Mahringer, who was photographed advising a somewhat nervous young actor, Richard Attenborough, balancing uneasily on skis while 'rehearsing for his new stage show *The Mousetrap*'). Another show business event in the store that year was an exhibition about the making of the film *Quo Vadis?*, a display opened by Peter Ustinov (who played Nero in the film). Another first for the store was the preparation and organisation of a Simpson fashion show at Ciro's club in the West End (one of the dancers dressed by Simpsons was the young Audrey Hepburn).

Early in December there were special evening parties at which (male) guests were provided with suggestions for Christmas presents, to be bought at the store's Gift Shop. These events were publicised as Men Only Parties (a title that dates the promotion: it could surely never be used in the 1990s). One year the theme was Racing; male customers were sent 'members' badges', and offered 'an odds-on selection of gifts, napped to please the fillies!'

In 1953, to mark the Queen's Coronation, there was a display of impressive replicas of the Crown Jewels. In the following year, the parent company could celebrate a special Royal event, when in October 1954 the Duke of Edinburgh toured the factory of S Simpson Limited at Larkhall outside Glasgow. The Duke was aware of Simpsons through his friendship with Major Huskisson: both were enthusiastic members of the Lord's Taverners (cricket enthusiasts who held their meetings at the Tavern at Lord's, – the purpose of the Taverners being to raise money for charity: the Duke accepted the accolade of Twelfth Man). The Larkhall factory had been opened in 1949 by the President of the Board of Trade, Harold Wilson (although a Simpson factory had been started in older buildings on the site, as part of the need to find manufacturing space outside London with the near-obliteration of the Stoke Newington factory by bombing). Larkhall was to become the manufacturing base, and Stoke Newington and another subsidiary factory in Nottingham (which had produced all DAKS women's wear) were eventually closed.

Prince Philip had now become a customer of Simpson Piccadilly, and in December 1954 the store received the Royal Warrant of Appointment as Outfitters to HRH The Duke of Edinburgh.

The store continued to be in the forefront of London fashion. Indeed, fashion shows were mounted in Simpsons. A report in the house magazine gives an idea of the acceptable styles of March 1956.

the sun and the shore,
call in and see
Simpson's sun-happy
beachwear
before you set out
for the South.

Beach and holiday clothes, 1957.

The *haute couture* collections are over and buyers have returned gleaming-eyed and undaunted, if a little exhausted, by the rigours endured in their hot-house atmosphere. Paris has waved her magic wand, and now madame can, in the more leisured atmosphere of the retail houses, see how its influence is going to affect the clothes she will wear in the months to come. Lines she may have thought of as impossibly extreme are subtly interpreted to become the darlings of the season.

In the Clover Room (the Simpson Piccadilly restaurant) this week the invited guests of Simpson's have been watching our Spring and Summer collection. It has included high fashion garments, classic suits and sportswear, and delicious play clothes in a brilliant bouquet of colours; so that women of very different personality, leading widely various lives, could all find clothes to interest them.

As the starting point of an English woman's wardrobe is so often a classic suit, we have shown several, notably a single-breasted beige gaberdine with the almost austere Savile-Row look dear to one section of our clientele. Another classic for which we have a great reputation is the camel coat: [we showed] a fine example by Leslie Raymond in 100 per cent camel hair.

More exciting - in that they contain an element of surprise - were the high fashion town clothes which formed the core of the collection. Sandra Russell's Langtry-like good looks gave an added fillip to Hardy Amies's crushed raspberry three-piece, and Jean Cumming wore Koupy's navy hopsack coat . . . The coat was taffeta-lined and canvas interlined, its tab fastenings and white pique cuffs making it a first cousin to some of the clothes shown in Paris the month before. The 'lingerie look' beloved of Dior and Mme. Fath made its appearance several times; Hardy Amies's navy suit was cuffed and collared in fondant pink, and his anthracite grey worsted coat and superb navy alpaca dress both had detachable white pique collar and cuffs . . .

The sheath dress, which achieves this summer's long-stemmed look appeared in several guises; one a mauve petalled shantung, another rose pattterned, and a third in white linen coin-spotted in hibiscus red. The camisole top, sometimes covered with the ubiquitous short jacket or bolero, if not new, is still a marked trend this season; one outstanding dress . . . was in a Sari-like material, striped gold and turquoise on cyclamen, its camisole top and hem banded in ribbon; another [was] in palest Della Robbia blue shantung.

Colour and fabrics this year have indeed been memorable; we showed a dirndl-type skirt printed with hot Van Gogh sunflowers, and a cotton bloomer suit in olive green had a wrap-round skirt printed with Capistrano roses. Particularly in the DAKS and play clothes was this colour trend so marked; one three piece was flamingo-pink, its blazer spiced with white stripes. We combined an electric 'Capri' blue with tangerine, and chartreuse with the new Capistrano rose.

The jersey suits were beautiful: one was a French jersey two-piece with a black-and-white jacquard top and plain black skirt, another was a sky-blue striped blazer and plain blue pleated skirt, and a third a navy jersey skirt with its three-quarter navy and white-striped coat and straw sailor straight from Renoir.

Golf and country clothes included faultlessly cut DAKS, some lovely twin-sets and heavy knits, and leather jackets. One white suede and heavy-knit jacket had its own white suede baker-boy beret; these were Florentine and worn with pillar-box red London slinkies.

Seafaring outfit, 1957. Simpson always
emphasised the practical for active sportswear.

Sea worthies

Be shipshape and Simpson fashion.
Left : Exclusive to Simpsons
PVC smock for really rough weather,
with lace-up front, and hood. Deep,
roomy pockets. £4.4.0. Inflator optional
£2.9.6. Matching PVC trousers. £2.5.0.

Right : Breton breaker
for sailing or the beach,
in lightweight proofed
sail cloth. In navy,
royal blue or Breton red.
Sizes 36-46. £2.7.6.
Jeans in the same cloth
and colours. Waist: 30-40;
leg length: 28-33. £3.7.6.

Simpson (Piccadilly) Ltd   *London W1 Regent 2002*

The collection showed a very lively awareness of high flight fashion trend, good workmanship, colour and design . . .

In 1956 the store was enlarged by increasing the frontage on Jermyn Street. Opened by Donald Campbell (son of Sir Malcolm Campbell who had opened the store 20 years earlier), the 'new building' consisted at first of two floors of offices for Simpson Piccadilly, and (on the fourth floor) a showroom for DAKS-Simpson, giving the manufacturing company a display space in central London (previously this function had been within the Stoke Newington factory). After manufacturing was centralised in Scotland, 34 Jermyn Street became the main offices of the parent company.

Associated with this development was a shop on the corner of Jermyn Street and Church Place. It has housed a number of Simpson Piccadilly departments, was for many years the 'DAKS Corner Shop', and in recent years has been the 'Studio' shop, appealing to younger men (and using the old logo of the Simpson tailoring company, the needle-and-thread 'S'). From this shop, along Jermyn Street to the eastern end of Simpsons, a line of display windows had been leased by Simpson Piccadilly for 20 years. Behind these windows were BBC recording studios (a continued use of the old theatre space, the wartime Stage Door Canteen). When these studios closed in 1975, J Lyons & Co as leaseholders were given permission by the Crown to demolish the studios and build shops on the site. Simpson decided to occupy the Jermyn Street half (now the Joseph shop).

The staff of Simpson Piccadilly possessed other distinctions. For not a few of them were distinguished athletes in their own right. In July 1952 Peter Elliott was diving in the Olympic Games at Helsinki. A few years later, and Brian Hewson was running for Britain in the Southern Games in the Caribbean, while Jennifer Middleton was taking part in the Wimbledon tennis tournament: a few years after that, Christine Truman (now Mrs G T Janes) earned still greater fame as a tennis champion. Joan Anderson was a member of the British Water-ski Team. The British Olympic teams were generally kitted out in DAKS trousers and skirts, and Simpson-tailored blazers. England cricket teams, at all levels, at home and abroad, have usually been kitted out by Simpsons, as have the England World Cup football teams of 1966, 1970, 1986 and 1990, and the England European Nations Championship teams of 1988 and 1992. The Paul Stewart racing team has also been supplied with clothing, taking Simpson Piccadilly into the circuits of motor racing.

The staff were hard worked - and at no time more than in the January sales, which year by year attracted record numbers of customers, and record takings. In January 1957, it was noted that 4,000 customers entered the store in the first ten minutes. On the first day of the sales, the doors had to be closed for a time, such was the press of people trying to enter. One salesman (Mr Diggin) took over £1,000 on the first day - and for the second year in succession.

The store had become a favoured port of call for leading figures in sport, politics, the arts and show business. A note was taken of some of the famous people of the day who had visited the store recently:

The Duchess of Gloucester; Mr Selwyn Lloyd [Foreign Secretary]; Sir William Grey [Chairman, Martins Bank]; Mr & Mrs Peter Sellers; Mr & Mrs Spike Milligan; Channing Pollock; Arthur Askey; Forrest Tucker; Jack Hylton; Mr & Mrs Bryan Forbes; Richard Attenborough; Ann Todd; Jean Seberg; Pat Kirkwood and Hubert Gregg; Julie Harris; Cyril Fletcher;

Dr Leonard Simpson.

Maureen Swanson; Pete Murray; Elsie & Doris Waters; Michael Medwin; Mr & Mrs George Cole; Richard Widmark; Dickie Henderson; Donald Houston; Donald Campbell; Victor Barna; Lord Hore-Belisha; Jill Bennett; Sir Laurence Olivier; John Pertwee; Tyrone Power; Jimmy Edwards; The Duke of Norfolk; Charles Coburn; Dirk Bogarde; Eric Sykes; Humphrey Lyttleton; Alma Cogan; Sir John Gielgud.

To those might be added other entertainers who were customers over the years: John Wayne, Bing Crosby, Frank Sinatra, Lana Turner, Tony Hancock and Sid James, and (the favourite of all Simpson staff who had the pleasure of serving him) Tommy Cooper. Martin Moss, then managing director, recalls escorting Marlene Dietrich through the store.

The 21st anniversary of the store in 1957 was marked in several ways. Dr Simpson commissioned a mural for the restaurant, of London seen from the South Bank, painted by John Spencer Churchill. Its unveiling was attended by Lady Churchill (a pleasant coincidence, since after Sir Winston Churchill's death in 1965, Dr Simpson was to buy at auction the Churchills' London home in Hyde Park Gate).

This anniversary was particularly significant for another reason. In November 1957 Lord Barnby, who had shouldered the chairmanship of the Simpson parent company and also of Simpson (Piccadilly) Limited on the death of Alec Simpson, was now in his 73rd year. His acceptance of the Chairmanship had enabled Dr Leonard Simpson to continue his distinguished career in medicine. But now after 21 years Lord Barnby felt it was time to retire. He handed over the control of the company to Dr Simpson, who at the age of 57 was able to reduce his medical commitments so as to spend yet more time with the family company. His fellow directors, and all the Simpson staff, well knew that in the years of his deputy chairmanship, Dr Simpson had been deeply concerned with the development of the store, and had initiated many of the most brilliant and successful ideas for its promotion. During the war, on top of his manifold medical responsibilities, he had acted as Director of Personnel and Consultant in Industrial Medicine and Industrial Psychology to the Simpson companies. He delighted in travel, and was personally involved in the sales success of DAKS abroad, particularly in America and Canada. Dr Simpson always managed to combine his business travels with visits to the world's golf courses. From November 1957 he was able to do all this as chairman of the family companies, including Simpson (Piccadilly) Limited.

For his part, Lord Barnby did not sink into a torpid retirement. He lived on for a further 25 years to the age of 98, and within a few weeks of his death was actively participating in field sports, and continuing to ride fearlessly. At Simpson Piccadilly he attended social events, and was from time to time to be seen walking round the store, cheerfully greeting the older sales staff by name, and eager to hear about the latest successes.

THE SIXTIES

For men country comfort meets Italian styling. (1-r) 1960, a sports worsted Kendal style in a "gun club" check; heavy Scottish tweed in Rutland style. The jackets are looser and longer than high fashion dictated but by 1962 the tighter shorter trouser meant that fashion was no longer something the smart man could easily take sitting down!

IN A *man's* WORLD

Simpson PICCADILLY

1960-61 the continental cut modified for a clientele used to comfort gave them a slimmer but still easy fitting jacket with loose natural shoulder line and long lapel and tapering trousers with deep ankle-high turn-up. (r) Hoff illustrated Oakham, a country suit with central jacket vent; Sackville, a business suit with a smart Robin Hood type hat; the latest version of the blazer, which was also available double breasted. Dinner jackets adapt to the client: slim fit, high button for the young. For the older man a return to the low lapel, loose cut of the forties and fifties. Sports clothes are given an American flavour: plus-twos for golf and moccasin styled slip-on shoes with the "standard" 1961 trouser.

In 1967 the classic Italian line: tight fitting, with short boxy jacket and restrictive low-rise drain-pipe trousers. The wool and mohair jacket with central vent is worn with a crew-neck sweater, the Shetland tweed window-pane check jacket with a roll-neck sweater. Also available mail order are new style accessories. Traditional Viyella adapted their standard check shirt to a closer cut and added a clingy roll-collar sweater to the range. Extrovert Carnaby Street subdued are the narrow Slim Jim tie and the frill fronted evening shirt.

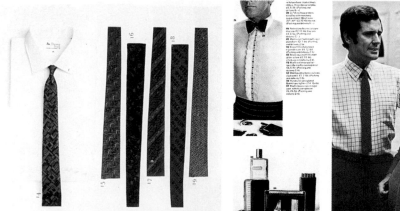

,

.

THE SIXTIES

Pop tailoring for Trend, the new young Simpson mini-shop, 1968, puts a Beatle lookalike in a neat Cardin type 1968 suit in terylene and wool featuring a long fitted jacket with a neat turn-down collar; A vegetarian version of the wild bunch 1971 wears a Quasar Khan outfit, with a quilted tweed bomber jacket trimmed with fake fur and a patterned jersey suit applied with suedette. The new fabrics, light terylene mixes and synthetic jerseys, contributed to the trim silhouette.

Trend at Simpson
PICCADILLY

Attenuated elegance, drawn by the new Simpson
fashion artist, Eric Stemp, was to transmogrify the form
fitting fashion from the later 1960s through the seventies
– informal Daks "companions", 1968; a "long lean"
lounge suit of 1969; a Daks top coat, 1969.

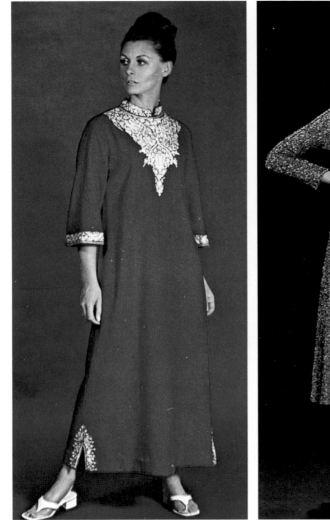

For ladylike hippies,
Simpson provided a wide range
of mail order picturesque. (above)
a maxi & a Holly Park lurex midi of
the late 1960s; (below) a suede
dolman jacket and skirt, 1972; a
psychedelic silk top, 1967.

Colour and pattern were fashion features from the late 1950s. (bottom l-r): a neo romantic "bather" with cover up cape by Lana of California in a "Tyrolian" print, 1963; a mix-match holiday wardrobe in a Spanish printed cotton in sub-modernist design, 1961; a late 1960s synthetic summer dress "carefree and crease resistant" with fashion conscious long pointed collar and short hemline. Daks Sleekers are now elasticated stretch pants. Spandex, the essential component, had only been introduced in 1959.

Designer promotions were a feature of the 1960s: (l) 1964, from the New York designer Bonnie Cashin a Cashmere intarsia twin-set with matching skirt. Cashin, well known for her countrified casuals, would have found this an attractive project and it reciprocated a Simpson Pringle cashmere promotion in New York.
(r) Clive of London designed the 1963 tweed coat and suit, a gentle version of the Parisian severe semi-fitted line of Cardin and Courrèges.

Elegance is natural

THE SIXTIES

1970 and modified minis, bland in colour needed new style accessories. Blunt-toed shoes and boxy bags in novelty patents were succeeded by a sleeker, sexier range of choices (bottom r) in 1974.

5

THE SWINGING SIXTIES

Young and Gay. Outfits inspired as much by Paris Courrèges as English Mary Quant.

As chairman of all the Simpson companies from November 1957, Dr Leonard Simpson continued to exercise a powerful influence on Simpson Piccadilly, which became his business base. He was frequently to be seen in the store, often with his wife and increasingly with their young daughter Georgina. He hosted innumerable public promotions and staff social events in the store, and was recognised as its extremely active chairman. In most years he would tour abroad (frequently combining his various interests in the course of such tours, particularly medicine, the export drives of the parent company, the promotion of Simpson Piccadilly to prospective visitors, and golf on the world's best courses). When in Britain he would be in the Store every week, meeting the managing directors of DAKS and Simpson Piccadilly on Tuesdays and Thursdays. Although these were informal meetings, an agenda of matters to be discussed was handed to 'Doctor' at the beginning of each session. In the last week of every month, board meetings were held: at 10.30 each morning he would appear on the sixth floor to chair meetings of Simpson Piccadilly on Tuesdays, the manufacturing company on Wednesdays, and the parent company S Simpson Limited on Thursdays, for which formal agendas would be circulated in advance. Dr Simpson's manner was precise, methodical and brisk. His approach to each item was rigorously thorough. A man who had throughout his medical life needed to be observant and accurate in diagnosis, he applied the same clear analysis to business. While he was actively sympathetic to the human problems and difficulties of individual members of staff, he was never prepared to tolerate time-wasting. Under his direction, the businesses were run with benevolent paternalism.

In 1959 Dr Simpson's 21st anniversary as a director of the store was marked by the board and senior staff with a dinner in his honour at Claridge's. That year was particularly eventful for the directors, since one of their number, Sir Harold Gillett, was elected Lord Mayor of London (a year later, he was pleased to attend a meeting in the store at which he, with eligible members of the staff, was presented with an engraved gold watch to mark his 21 years of service).

The style of the store was definitively 'English', countrified, and proud of it. Pride was understandable when at New Year 1962 Simpson Piccadilly received the Royal Warrant as Outfitters to HM The Queen, joining that of the Duke of Edinburgh awarded six years earlier. A series of senior salesmen from Simpson Piccadilly had the responsibility of taking merchandise to Buckingham Palace to show to the Queen and the Duke. The first was G G Griffiths: 'Griff' was a popular character in the West End, maintaining contact with foreign Embassies and the major hotels, and developing a steady flood of overseas visitors to the store. He was

Sleekers, 1959.

succeeded as salesman to the Palace by Alf Huggins, and then by 'Mr Tenby'. His name, in fact, was Oswald Lewis; but when he joined Simpson Piccadilly in 1946 it was the custom that no two members of the staff could use the same name, and there was already a 'Mr Lewis' on the staff. So he chose the 'store name' of Tenby, because he had happy memories of childhood holidays there. Years later, when made a Member of the Victorian Order (the Queen's personal order for service to the Royal Family), he was gazetted as 'Mr Lewis', and the Queen asked why. He explained the reason; and the Queen said that she would like to continue to call him 'Mr Tenby', if he didn't mind, because that was how she had thought of him for so long. On his retirement, he was succeeded by yet another Welshman, John Bayliss (subsequently general manager of Simpson Piccadilly).

The Queen's Royal Warrant was the ultimate accolade for the store as the authoritative source of traditional British style. A Simpson marketing executive, after visiting a European trade show of the latest men's fashions, reported with scarcely veiled distaste:

> There were several examples of what I will call 'extremist' clothing: a suit in pure silk; the notorious [Italian] 'Vittorio' suit with its abbreviated length, four-button fastening, and diminutive lapels; a collarless smoking jacket in star-spangled crimson silk; and a violently coloured yachting outfit consisting of a bright blue sweater with a non-tarnishable thread running through it, coral pink slacks, and bright blue leather shoes. These were amusing oddities, but I presume to say that their importance as regards the overall picture in men's clothing is but slight. They are perhaps a pointer to the new colour-consciousness in men's fashions, but I predict that they will take a very long time to achieve full acceptance by the average British male.

That was written in 1956. Within a very few years, things were to change. An acknowledgement of that was the opening of a new department on the fourth floor offering fashions for younger women, and named (a title that could never have been applied even a decade later) 'Young and Gay'. In September 1958 Simpson Piccadilly became the first West End London store to mount a major fashion show in a London hotel. In the ballroom of Grosvenor House, Park Lane two thousand invited guests watched a colourful parade of men's and women's fashions for autumn and winter, including ski-wear. For women, the Empire line was featured in mohair and Courtelle, with DAKS skirts and (an innovation) 'Sleekers', DAKS slacks with a narrow cut 'but not over-tight'. There was also a range of active and après-ski clothes in bright colours, together with DAKS elasticised ski trousers. For men, suits had a slim silhouette: jackets with narrower lapels. The show launched a short topcoat and, for wear in town, 'the new lightweight bowler'. For country wear, there was a soft tweedy hat 'à la Rex Harrison'. The main colour was blue, 'teamed with a crisp white or white ground shirt, possibly striped'. In the country, the Simpson man would wear DAKS 'Chiltern' trousers, with slanting cross-pockets and raised side seams: an assortment of sweaters, sports shirts and jackets were matched with the DAKS.

The show was a great success, and a second version was held at Grosvenor House in the following spring. This had to be repeated on six successive evenings, and was still 'standing room only'. A new style was introduced for DAKS suits, with a soft shoulder line and narrower lapels. For leisure wear, 'twin sets for men' were introduced, and Norfolk jackets returned (inspired by Prince Philip). In these shows, some of the staff

The famous Simpson Christmas tree of lights –
see also page *viii*.

joined the professional models, and the *Daily Mail* fashion writer
particularly liked 'a shortish middle-aged man [Ken Perry] with a gentle
smile . . . He looked cosy, better than the tall handsome boys.' Hats were
designed by students of the Royal College of Art. There was also a notable
display of European wear, chosen by Simpson's fashion consultant Mme.
Françoise Garrigues: 'Rainwear from Belgium, beachwear from France,
suede from Italy, scarves and swimsuits from Switzerland, coat-and-skirt
ensembles from Austria, weather styles from Denmark, and in addition to
the famed DAKS features, Britain was represented in Ascot styles, suits,
tennis wear, Scotch tweeds and Irish hand-woven linens.'

The Grosvenor House fashion shows were organised by a brilliant
display executive, Martin Christopherson, assisted by Peter Southgate (who
later succeeded him). Their influence on design and display at Simpson
Piccadilly was profound, continuing the innovation and excitement dating
back to the architect Joseph Emberton, carried forward by his assistant
Rodney Thomas, and upheld during and after the war by Natasha Kroll. It
was Miss Kroll who invented the great Christmas tree of lights, stretching
all the way down the Piccadilly frontage. The idea was developed each year
by Christopherson, one of the most successful being that of 1961 when the
Piccadilly facade and the ground floor were decorated with 5,000 silver
'witch balls', more than 200 Christmas trees, 9,500 pinhead lights, 500
yards of specially woven fabric, and branches of blue pine, a considerable
challenge for the maintenance team under Fred Clenshaw to assemble. A
number of customers tried to buy the decorations.

The Simpson fashion shows became part of the social calendar, being
strongly promoted by the publicity manager H Stafford-Northcote. The
presentation in 1959 (when Simpsons became a founder member of the
British Menswear Guild) was opened by the Minister of State at the Board
of Trade, Frederick Erroll (later Lord Erroll). He made the point that

> DAKS and the Simpson organisation have always played their part
> magnificently in Britain's export drive . . . Sometimes we are given the
> impression that casual clothes are a recent importation from abroad. We

Ground floor display for the Best of Britain
promotion, Jermyn Street entrance.

DAKS skirts, 1961. Good cut compensates for
brevity for this new free-wheeling life style.

know better. We know it was a man called Alexander Simpson who stripped
us of our grey flannel bags which were held precariously aloft by means of a
slippery belt, and poured us into beautifully tailored DAKS which
miraculously stayed up on their own.

As the *Evening Standard* commented: 'Simpsons of Piccadilly, veterans of
the battle to persuade Englishmen to wear something brighter than a dark
grey suit, staged another offensive against conservative tailoring at
Grosvenor House . . .' At this show, there was particular applause for the
official uniform of the British team for the Olympic Games: a DAKS blazer
and DAKS trousers or skirts.

Indeed, as the Trade Minister had said, a considerable export success
had already been achieved in North America: the parent company were to
launch a subsidiary company, DAKS USA, in 1963, and DAKS shops were
opened on the transatlantic liners *Queen Mary* and *Queen Elizabeth*, the
sales staff supplied from Simpson Piccadilly. It was a very popular duty: two
members of staff who happily recall their cruises across the Atlantic from
Southampton to New York are Michael Bowen (later to be successful as a
men's merchandise executive), and Bill Read. Simpson were the first to
capitalise on the possibilities in the Italian market for men's knitwear. (In
June 1959 the store lost two of its most promising managers when John
Palmer (advertising) and Percy Charles Nichols (display) were killed in an
air crash outside Milan, while on their way to study the Italian menswear
market on behalf of Simpson Piccadilly: both were in their early 40s, and
had been marked out for promotion.)

Other export markets in which Simpson led the way were Spain and
Scandinavia. Simpsons were the biggest exporter of British men's wear,
and by 1966 could claim that sales to Europe had multiplied five-fold in ten
years. It was a two-way traffic: at this time Simpson Piccadilly began to
import continental merchandise of outstanding quality, and earned great
respect from foreign suppliers for the store's merchandising skills which
were generally regarded as leading the West End - not least through the
work of B A Keeling, later a director, who was responsible for much of the
store's merchandising success (he was married to Mary Buck, the highly
effective personnel manager). Among other foreign imports, the Simpson
spring fashion show at Grosvenor House featured resort wear by Elio
Berhanyer, a young Spanish designer employing 'the vividly clear, hot
colourings of the Iberian peninsula'. It was the decade in which British
tourists began to flock in thousands to the Spanish sun; there was a special
store promotion, Costa del Sol Week, staged to mark the inauguration of
direct flights by British European Airways and Iberia Airways between
London and Malaga (Dr Simpson launched the promotion in fluent
Spanish, at a reception in the store).

Throughout the sixties, Simpson Piccadilly continued to mount special
promotions for the major sporting events of the social calendar. In the
spring there was the boat show, in summer there was Wimbledon and the
Test matches, in the autumn there were exhibitions linked to the Royal
International Horse Show at Wembley, followed by skiing and winter
sports. The Horse Show was a particular interest of the Simpson family,
since Mrs Simpson was a horse-owner, and Dr and Mrs Simpson's
daughter Georgina was earning a notable reputation as a show jumper (in
1960 alone she won 15 junior open jumping competitions). Simpson
Piccadilly introduced the first dry ski slope to London, with a new ski

Sports clothes. 1974. The pocket feature is an imaginative up-dating of traditional styling.

[From TREND Autumn 1976] The 21st Wimbledon Tennis Reception was held in the store in June 1976. A toast was proposed by Sir Roger Bannister, who then (with Mrs Georgina Andrews) cut a cake baked and decorated in the Simpson kitchen by Chef Charles.

department on the sixth floor in a Swiss chalet: the ski slope itself was set up in the Westminster Ballroom in Stratton Ground, where it was featured on both BBC and Independent Television.

In 1962, Simpson Piccadilly added to its successful promotion of classic English styling for men by opening a new department devoted to the younger fashions for men that were being introduced by imaginative young designers: 'Trend for Men' was managed by a young designer from this school, Gordon Deighton.

Dr Simpson's favourite sport continued to be golf; from his student days in America he had become familiar with famous American courses. Later he actively promoted Anglo-American competitions, and in 1961 he inaugurated the Walter Hagen Award, a massive silver cup to be presented annually to a golfer who in the opinion of the members of the Golf Writers' Association of America best exemplified 'the epic character of the impact of the great Walter Hagen on Anglo-American golf and especially the Ryder Cup competition, in which he was captain no less than seven times; and the vital importance in this day and age of Anglo-American friendship, understanding and solidarity in world affairs'. In April 1961 Dr Simpson presented the cup to the great Walter Hagen himself, in Chicago. He then boarded a plane and arrived back in London in order to attend a reception in the Simpson Services Club for Royal International Horse Show competitors, including Pat Smythe and Lady Sarah Fitzalan-Howard, who had won the Queen Elizabeth II cup. (The John Player Cup, a gold horse's head, was displayed in the store window throughout the week.) It was a busy year, for another reception was held for the Wimbledon players; 347 guests attended, including the Australian Test cricket team. The DAKS Ladies' International Golf Tournament took place in May, and the DAKS Golf Tournament in June, both at Wentworth.

There was also an annual reception in the store for members of the Torch Trophy Trust, an organisation established in 1962 by the man who organised the relay of runners to carry the Olympic Torch from Greece to the London Olympic Games in 1948. The charity exists to encourage voluntary work for sport at grass roots level, by giving acknowledgement to people who have given such service and received no recognition. Some 25 recipients are thanked in this way each year, and presented with a miniature replica of the Olympic Torch. The first chairman was Lord Porritt (who had been a medical colleague of Dr Simpson at St Mary's Paddington). His successor Sir Colin Cowdrey was succeeded as chairman by Ted Croker, former Secretary of the Football Association. The work of many other charities has been assisted by special events held in the store, including St Dunstan's (the home for disabled servicemen), King George's Fund for Sailors, the National Playing Fields Association, the Save the Children Fund, and the NSPCC (to which the profits of a Christmas shopping evening were donated), as well as clothing industry charities.

Through these years Simpson Piccadilly was fortunate to have a group of senior executives most of whom had grown up with the store and worked together for a number of years. They were led by 'Freddie' Brame, who had been appointed managing director in 1959 when Major Alfred Huskisson had been promoted to deputy chairman of the parent company. Freddie Brame had been a trusted lieutenant to Alec Simpson at Stoke Newington, and had been invited to the store to resolve its teething troubles soon after the opening in 1936. It was to become his life. Tall, elegant, a keen cricketer and enthusiastic if imperfect golfer, he was supported by a dedicated staff. The general manager was 'Reggie' Cross, finance executive Albert 'B' Burton, personnel executive Mary Buck (who married the Men's Merchandise Manager Bernard Keeling), with G G Griffiths, George Cook and Mr Alf Huggins. Evelyn Whiteside had returned after some years at Fortnums to be Women's Merchandise Executive, a figure of immense elegance and distinction, admired throughout the trade for her impeccable appearance on all occasions - never a hair out of place. She was matched in elegance and charm by Margaret (Maggie) Engel-Hansen, Women's Marketing Executive. At this time the Men's Marketing Manager was the irrepressible Jack Creed, who had earlier been a brilliant 'welcomer' on the ground floor, where he seemed to know every customer by name. Among his 'special customers' was the royal family of Monaco; in 1977 Simpson Piccadilly received the warrant of appointment to HSH Prince Rainier.

On his retirement in 1978 Bernard Keeling's responsibilities for store merchandising were carried forward by Michael Bowen, who at his retirement as Men's Merchandise Executive in 1992 concluded 42 years of dedicated and effective service to the store. Mary Buck was succeeded as Personnel Executive by Morag Golesworthy: in a remarkable example of longevity of service, the store has had only three personnel managers in its 60 years.

In the mid-sixties, on the retirement of Major Huskisson as managing director of S Simpson Limited, Dr Simpson asked Freddie Brame to take over the direction of the parent company. At the same time, it became clear to 'Doctor' and Freddie Brame that in the spirit of the day it would be good if new ideas from outside the company could be introduced in the direction of Simpson Piccadilly. In 1966 (the year that the England football team won the World Cup, and Simpsons provided their off-field kit) Martin Moss was appointed deputy managing director, to succeed Freddie Brame in the following year. Martin Moss was then 43; he had earned a notable reputation in modernising Woollands of Knightsbridge and Debenham & Freebody. He admired the combination of tradition and innovation that was characteristic of Simpsons. He had an awareness of the importance of design in industry (appointed CBE for his work as deputy chairman of the Design Council, he was in 1982 nominated to the Royal Fine Art Commission). As a member of the Council of the Royal College of Art, he admired the design standards that had been set by Alec Simpson within the building and merchandise, but he also recognised that while the store was a remarkable example of the advanced styles of the thirties, it needed to attract a new young clientele. With the appointment of Martin Moss to manage Simpson Piccadilly, Freddie Brame moved to become managing director of the parent company, S Simpson Limited, and also deputy chairman. At the same time, the family participation in the companies was demonstrated by the appointment of Johnny Mengers as deputy managing director of S Simpson Limited. Johnny Mengers was half-brother of Mrs Heddy Simpson, and had joined the Simpson manufacturing company on the design side after a training in cutting and designing. He was admired in the trade for his imaginative promotion of DAKS products, particularly in export markets round the world, where his fluency in French, German, Italian and Spanish was as useful as his flair for clothing design.

Though Martin Moss also admired the tradition of DAKS, he was certain that Simpson Piccadilly needed to attract more customers through good publicity. In 1967 and 1968 there was a series of lively promotions in the

Frederick Brame.

Gary Player, 1977.

Romantic revival sports clothes feature an
Inverness cape, 1978.

Store. The first was Scotland '67, in which exhibits from Scottish industry
were displayed on each floor of Simpsons. The exhibition was opened by
the Rt Hon William Ross, then Secretary of State for Scotland. The growing
off-shore oil industry was well represented, together with the Scottish
Tourist Board and the National Trust for Scotland. This was a particularly
appropriate enterprise for Simpsons, since the parent company's
manufacturing base was now totally centralised in a modern custom-built
factory at Larkhall on the outskirts of Glasgow. Over the years new
computer technologies were introduced, until Larkhall became one of the
largest and most up-to-date factories for the manufacture of clothing in the
world. (A decade later, in 1979, it was to be visited by the Queen and Prince
Philip.) The Group's production capacity was increased by the purchase of
Invertère, an old-established manufacturer of fine quality rainwear and
also the reversible coat. With the expansion of its factory at Newton Abbot,
Devon, the company widened its ranges to include casual outerwear coats
in modern styles, which have been marketed successfully under the brand
name Invertère Coatwrights at home and abroad.

In 1967, Sir Francis Chichester circumnavigated the world in record
time in his small boat *Gipsy Moth*. On his return, there was another special
exhibition in Simpson Piccadilly, and the parent company launched a new
range of 'Chichester' sailing kit, of DAKS jersey wool trousers and 'bridge'
coats. 1967 was a good year for sport, since another DAKS promotion
featured the golf champion Gary Player, who visited the store to act as
coach in the Golf Clinic. In the following year, the area on the fifth floor
that had been occupied by the Simpson Services Club, with its magnificent
balcony view over London, was redesigned by Rodney Fitch as a new
department for women's holiday wear, furnished with a coffee bar, and
named the Summer House. In the autumn, there was the now customary
Euro-Ski exhibition. The next year was similarly full of new promotions. In
March, a show of *Punch* cartoons on the subject of flying, to mark the 50th
anniversary of the RAF, was opened by David Langdon, and a reception
was attended by Air Marshal Sir Dermot Boyle. In contrast, in April an
exhibition of photographs of the Royal Danish Ballet (then in London) was
visited by the King and Queen of Denmark. The *Observer* sponsored a
series of fashion shows in the store, attracting a young clientele to the
Trend shop for men, and the Young and Gay department for women. As a
further encouragement to the young, Simpsons sponsored a bursary for
clothing design at the Royal College of Art. The Wimbledon reception in
the store, traditionally held on the first Wednesday of Wimbledon fortnight,
was attended by the young star 'Gorgeous Gussie' Moran and the British
hope Roger Taylor. (Gussie gave tennis tips on the second floor.) This was
the year in which Wimbledon was opened for the first time to professional
players as well as amateurs. The Simpson receptions continued to be a
featured social event during Wimbledon for some years longer (in 1972,
Clark Graebner and Ilie Nastase were both photographed wearing suits
from the Simpson men's boutique, Trend). Gradually the stars of tennis, as
with other sports, began to put a price on their appearances at social
events, and such gatherings as the Simpson party for Wimbledon
competitors came to an end.

In 1968 the London stores, with the two 'local' newspapers, the *Evening
Standard* and *Evening News*, mounted the first Festival of London Stores.
On Whit Monday there was a great procession through the west end, with
floats provided by each of the major stores. The Simpson float, Going to

A Simpson bus ran round London during the Festival of London Stores 1970, sponsored by the *Evening Standard* and the *Evening News*, two of whose young journalists, Frankie McGowan and Peter Cole, are on the platform. Upstairs is the guest group of the day, Deep Purple.

Mars, was a great success (the first man was to step on to the moon a year later), and backed up with a 'Pickadilly' display in the store opened by Noël Coward. The first 'Miss London Stores' was Ruth Hitchcock of Simpson Piccadilly (later to marry Simpson executive Don Ruffle). In the following year, Simpsons once again triumphed: the store's training officer, Penny Webster, was voted the second 'Miss London Stores' (and won a trip to Tokyo to take part in a British Week there). In 1970 the theme was 'Pop on a Bus', and involved a number of young pop groups.

These promotions were supported with vigorous advertising campaigns: the store's advertising was now in the hands of Vernon Stratton. Although Eric Stemp had succeeded Max Hoff as the artist producing the traditional sketches of elegant men that had come to epitomise Simpson style from the opening of the store, and continued to produce drawings in this style, it was decided to add photography and to use a single model for the advertisements who would become known as 'the Simpson man': for a number of years Brewster Blackmer occupied this role. There were other store promotions at this time, notably the 'Fine Finland' exhibition which was shared with Heals: each store introduced modern Finnish merchandise from the other, and the result was in each case effective and profitable.

*   *   *

In 1969 the Simpson group was radically reorganised, notably with the creation of a new subsidiary, DAKS-Simpson Limited, to be responsible for the manufacturing and marketing of DAKS clothes. S Simpson Limited thereafter became the holding company of the group, with four subsidiary companies in Britain (the others being Simpson (Piccadilly) Limited, Jermyn Street Selections Limited, and the Invertère Coat Company Limited), and three overseas (Simpson Imports Inc. USA, DAKS USA Limited, and DAKS Canada Limited). The Invertère Coat Company had been purchased by S Simpson in 1966; the company received the Queen's Award to Industry in 1968 for its exports.

Simpson Piccadilly was listed as a building of special architectural and historic interest in 1970, a special though posthumous tribute to Joseph Emberton, the architect, and Alexander Simpson, the client. The Simpson group, and with it Simpson Piccadilly, celebrated Freddie Brame's election as Master of the Worshipful Company of Woolmen, the City Livery Company, in 1971-72. Unfortunately, the staff at Simpson Piccadilly had to cope for several years with an increasing number of day-to-day problems that were caused by external political factors : power cuts, which meant that there were occasions when the store was lit by candle-light, until sufficient generators could be purchased and installed. And then, from 1973, a bombing campaign in central London by the IRA meant that additional security measures had to be introduced, and all staff trained in their use. Additionally, and most serious for a store such as Simpson Piccadilly that attracted many overseas visitors, Americans chose not to include London on their holiday itineraries. The effect on the financial results of the store was very significant.

Nevertheless, the old traditions were upheld. Each year the chef made more than 1,000 Simpson Christmas Puddings, based on a 19th-century recipe; the majority were sold in the restaurant, many to overseas visitors, though each year the staff generally bought about 300.

In 1973 Martin Moss, with some regret, resigned as managing director of Simpson Piccadilly to become chief executive of a leading group of department stores in the United States. The store was now in the charge of Jack Creed and Leslie Parker as deputy managing directors. Nevertheless, there were plenty of Simpson staff for whom the store was a lifetime occupation. There were still some staff at Simpson Piccadilly who had been there from the opening day (though many had been in the services during the war). A typical record was that of W J 'Bill' Millard (who died in 1969 aged 80): he had been stationed at the Piccadilly entrance from the store's opening until his retirement at the end of 1966, the first person everyone met on entering Simpson Piccadilly, a familiar burly figure to the great and the famous, and every ordinary customer, to all of whom he was Simpson's 'welcomer'. To the staff he was Father Christmas at many of Major Huskisson's parties for their children.

On the 37th anniversary of the store in 1973 it was noted that in the previous 16 years, 103 gold watches for long service had been presented to the staff of the Simpson Group, and 53 recipients were still working in the store.

Autumn, 1967.

FIRE! Daks Companions fire your imagination and set the Autumn alight with their new colours of Burnt Orange, Smoked Jade and Ash Blue. Daks Companions feature Shetland and Lambswool sweaters and silk shirts perfectly partnered with a variety of exclusively designed tweeds.

Styles: Midhurst suit with silk shirt. Weston skirt *flared* and Sandown skirt *pleated* all in Shetland Tweed, with matching crew neck sweaters.

DAKS
SIMPSON LONDON TAILORED
at better shops everywhere or write to 34 Jermyn Street SW1

wool

Left to right: 1. Jeanne Marc smock dress in earth colours with padded bodice. £95. Small/medium/large. Exclusive to us in the U.K. 2. Man's suit. Jacket, brown/cinnamon tweed with brown wool trousers. £160. Cord blouson-style beige shirt £35. Viyella beige shirt £35. 3. Mandy Pothecary skirt with overblouse. Skirt £33. Top £42. Sizes 8-14. Also by the same designer: pencil-slim trousers £24 with matching top £46. All in cream embossed silk.

Simpson
JERMYN STREET

We reveal startling new goings on in Jermyn Street.

For famous names, exclusive names, high fashion
has a brand new name, Simpson Jermyn St.
At Simpson's new Jermyn St. shop, you'll meet the
names that are making the news now.
People like Walter Albini for Trell, Brigitte Bardot,
Scarlett Speedwell, Ninivah, Yves Saint Laurent
and many more, many of them exclusive to Simpson.
For men and women, fashion today is all a
matter of who you know.
Bursting with the brightest ideas, Simpson Jermyn St
is exactly the kind of exciting, constantly changing
shop that fashion needs this instant. So why not meet
your friends in our coffee shop, and then have
a browse. To see what's going on, get in there. Today.
Cream double breasted dinner jacket in pure wool £89
Black dress trousers in wool/mohair £39. Striped Cream
and black shirt in crepe de chine £48. Chris Clyne
culottes £64, shawl £32 in cream silk with frog
motif. Sizes 10-12.

Simpson
JERMYN ST

Simpson
PICCADILLY

1978 a characteristic
promotion for the new
Jermyn Street shop

New shop designed by David Hicks.

For those who can:

THE SEVENTIES

1971: the **Mary Quant** range, raunchy and romantic. (centre) hotpants or "playshorts and top", with a strawberry central and ripe for the plucking; (1) a dress with shoulder emphasis intended as military not militant; (r) a flutter with romance. British-born Mary Quant established the new young Chelsea look with her shop, Bazaar, opened in 1954. By 1966 she had pioneered an international revolution in young styling. (below) On the beach, 1979, and the line relaxes with easy fit exotic clothes.

Hot summer days...

THE SEVENTIES

Romantic reaction, and the Peacock
Revolution brought radical new styling to the Simpson range from the late 1960s. 1973 and Eric Stemp dresses his fairy-tale people in fantasy outfits, the women in floaty floral voiles, timeless tartans or nightmare psychedelics; the men in pseudo period suits, with Byronic frills and sleeves. The suit line had developed from the neat tight-fitting Cardin suit of the mid 1950s, and the high set sleeve had grown a padded peaked shoulder, balanced by broad lapels and the drain-pipe trousers a bell bottom flare. Colour and pattern are all-important.

2A. Her black velvet
jacket. 10–14. £19·50.
2B. Long Courtelle
tartan skirt. 10–14. £15·00.
2C. Frothy blouse.
10–14. £8·75.
2D. His velvet check
jacket. Grey/red/white
or black/emerald/
turquoise/pink
checks. £29·00.
2E. Velvet
trousers. Grey,
black, brown,
bottle, wine
or mink.
£11·75.

3A. Printed wool dress. As
shown or in mainly mid blue
background. 10–16. £28·00.
Tutankhamen inspired
coloured pendants.
3B. Large £5·75
3C. Small £2·50
CALÈCHE eau
de Toilette
3D. 220 cc £5·95
3E. 480 cc £8·95

6A. His INVERTÈRE wool and cashmere coat
with an alpaca collar. £64·00.
6B. His DAKS weekend two-piece wool suit.
Brown multi checks. £41·00.
6C. Pack easy overnight case. Beige or red. £19·50.

Her pigskin sueded trouser suit ha
acrylic pile lining and collar
Dark brown
7A. Jacket £68·50
7B. Trousers £35·00
7C. Leather and suede bag
Brown/beige or brown. £12·00
7D. Platform leather boots wit
shiny finish. Black or brown
3½–7½. £28·00
7E. Three flasks in novel leather
case. £7·00

4A. His nylon anorak. Flame red. £34·00.
4B. Wool/Helanca/Lycra ski trousers.
Navy, black or brown. £18.00.
4C. Her skunk/suede coat. £160·00.
4D. Ski trousers in wool/nylon/Lycra.
White, gold, red, navy or black. 8–18. £17·00.
4E. Wool balaclava. White, yellow
or red. £4·25.

THE SEVENTIES

1973 and sports clothes diversify when new colours and fabrics enter the range. (below) Tennis fashions by German designer Head exploit the possibilities of Dacron for durable prettiness. The skinny rib shirt is in cowboy style.

THE SEVENTIES

The late 1960s and the pared-down elegance of the Cardin-type unisex tunic and waistcoat suits contrasts with the loose-fitting Hippy exotica. Pity the ecologically correct Jesurum cotton (near r) is twice the price of the Rosemarie Reid polyester dress and the matching bathing suit in elastane and polymide.

THE SEVENTIES

For the more conventional
of 1971, there is fit and flare for the
men and for the women, the skirt has
grown from mini to midi.

Home and Away: during the 1970s and Simpson widens its options. (1-r) his and hers sweater, 1976, vividly conventional in modish 1920s style; unstructured post hippy fashion, with a safari style suit and a decolté gipsy dress. Brewster Blackmer, the Simpson man of the 1970s in the perfect formal 1972 suit, avocado striped, with waistcoat, broad lapels, tapered waist and flared trousers. The accessories are impeccable from the broad brimmed fur felt hat, the Windsor knot tie, the 4 button cuff and unexpectedly informal slip on casual moccasin type shoe. (bottom) slightly more informal with shapely 3 button jacket and tapering flat fronted trousers. The close fitting jacket sleeve focussed attention on the cuff link. The "semi brogue" shoes have changed little since the 1930s.

(opposite) **1978 an anti-trad promotion for the new Jermyn Street shop.** Here stylist Patsy Blane and photographer Graham Hughes confront a horrified pin striped city gent Leslie Phillips with an upmarket peasant in tiered cotton.

THE SEVENTIES

Holiday wear ranged from the techno to the tropical. (above) 1974 ski clothes in tergal and cotton, warm light and streamlined; (below) brief cotton bikini with a patchwork printed cover up.

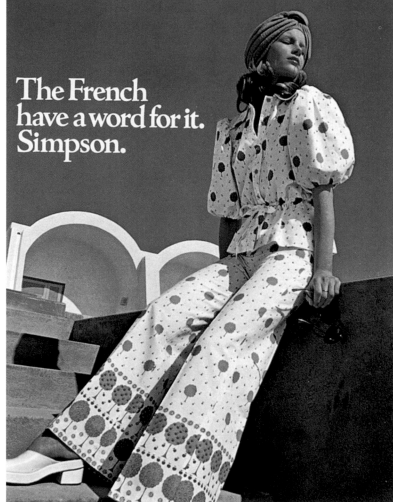

1972: unisex fit and flares, with a provocative Windsor knot tie. Colours had never been brighter. 1978: craft revival peasant, a patchwork printed caftan by Jean Marc. (below) The designer trouser suit with flared pants and platform soled shoes.

1975: Brewster models a check suit. Good cut was imperative when patterns were large and fit demanding. Her suit is similar in line. Boots had covered many a gap in the miniskirted 60s and remained in fashion even though the midi was the early 1970s standard skirt length. 1976: another lighthearted recall of the 1920s from the wide brimmed Fedora type hat to the two tone shoes; 1975; a new style patterned shirt, 1979. Too tight jackets and low rise hipster trousers made a flamboyant shirt a useful distraction from the occasional bulge or misfit. (below) 1979: middle of the road styling: a zip up windcheater jacket, still in vogue after thirty years.

(opposite): **Eric Stemp** brings his invariable elegance to his Portrait of Fashion promotion 1971; (l-r): a safari style wool sport jacket; a "Trail Blazer", new in fit and colour; (below) a formal lounge suit and Kipper tie, usually arranged in a double or Windsor knot to balance the broad lapels and deep collared shirts.

THE SEVENTIES

Knitted two piece
with overtunic by Clutch Cargo
Photographed at the Savoy Hotel

Modish British make believe: (l-r) the Sherlock Holmes Look 1977, with deerstalker cap and Inverness cape. A straight recall of turn of the century styling it remained popular for export promotions. 1977 and a US Clutch Cargo dress posed enigmatically in the Savoy. Moody, narrative fashion photography was becoming a feature of the decade. Trend and Young and Gay, 1971. Carefree fashion from the new department opened 1958 except that the pale colours so fashionable in the late 1960s early 1970s took a deal of looking after. (below) 1971 and the perfect Peacock male, in fairy tale velvet and frills.

6

NEW GENERATION

[From TREND Autumn 1976] To mark Dr Simpson's devotion to the cause of golf, and international understanding particularly between Great Britain and the United States, the golf writers of America awarded the Walter Hagen Trophy to Dr Simpson. The customary miniature given to each year's winner was presented to him at a reception in the Store by Henry Longhurst, a former winner and golf commentator.

From the mid-70s the nation's fortunes began to revive, and with them those of Simpson Piccadilly. An international note was struck at the Winter Sports reception of 1975 (attended by Prince Michael of Kent) when tourist bureaux and bars were installed in the store by the French, Austrian, Finnish and Italian tourist offices, staffed by girls in national costumes. In March 1976 a 22-ft model of the new Anglo-French supersonic airliner Concorde was shown on the ground floor (and the chef produced a celebratory crêpe named after it, which was offered to diners in the restaurant). It was a good year also for the association between Simpson Piccadilly and sport, since the Golf Writers of America voted to award the Walter Hagen cup to its initiator, Dr Leonard Simpson, in recognition of his services to golf and Anglo-American friendship (in addition to his golf associations, he was an advisory counsellor to the English Speaking Union). The cup was presented to Dr Simpson by Henry Longhurst, at a reception in the store. In the following year the store was specially decorated to celebrate the Queen's Silver Jubilee, and among special receptions were those to mark the London visit of the Spanish Riding School of Vienna, and a winter skiing reception attended by the British Olympic Ski Team. (Simpsons kitted out the British bobsleigh team which won the gold medal at the Winter Olympics at Innsbruck.)

But great changes were on the way. A new generation of the Simpson family was beginning to take part in the direction of Simpson Piccadilly. Dr Simpson had encouraged his daughter Georgina to take an interest in the Store and attend, with him and his wife Heddy, many social events organised by and for the staff. She had been brought up to recognise the family responsibility to be concerned for the wellbeing of their employees. In 1976 she was appointed an associate director, and became a director in the following year. With her husband, the actor Anthony Andrews, she had already begun to propose ideas for attracting more people of her own age into the store (and to that end had, a year or two earlier, hosted a reception to launch a book of photographs of that generation, Nobs and Nosh, by the young portrait photographer Allan Warren).

The display standards of Simpson Piccadilly continued to lead the trade, and to be an endless source of innovation and surprise. In 1977, to mark the Silver Jubilee of the Queen's accession to the throne, the whole of the ground floor was transformed into a garden, with flowers and lawns, fountains and seats. This promotion, in association with *Harper's and Queen*, received great acclaim.

Some years earlier the redevelopment of the block of buildings to the west of Simpsons in Jermyn Street in 1956 had made possible the opening of a shop on the corner of Church Place, beside St James's Church,

Penelope Keith opens Simpson Jermyn Street in March 1978. As Georgina Andrews was doing a radio interview, her dog Albert stood (or sat) in to represent the Simpson family.

The 'Simpson Check' of camel, vicuna and black (two of the most luxurious fibres, with black for contrast) was devised by Johnny Mengers, chairman of the Simpson Group, in 1984

Piccadilly. This had been used for a variety of purposes over the years: initially called Breakaway, it specialised in holiday and sports wear appropriate to the season. In the late '70s it became possible to extend Simpsons' occupancy of ground and first-floor properties on Jermyn Street so as to 'in-fill' Simpson visibility on that street virtually from the original shop, west to the corner shop on Church Place. It happened that at the time, the fashionable designer David Hicks had opened a shop on Jermyn Street across the road from Simpsons, and at the request of Mrs Heddy Simpson and her daughter Georgina, he was invited to design the new areas that would be available. Georgina Simpson began actively to promote new younger fashions for women, to complement the classic styles being offered at Simpson Piccadilly by Eve Bell as Women's Merchanise Director. She and Georgina Andrews made several forays to New York, and as a result Simpson Piccadilly became one of the the first West End stores to feature the latest womens' fashions from the USA. This search for the best of innovative fashions worldwide was continued by Sally Hunter as Women's Merchandise Executive, and later as a director of the store.

Simpson Jermyn Street (No.32) was opened (by Penelope Keith) on 15th March 1978. A notable feature was the number of fashionable international designer names on display - Walter Albini for Trell, Brigitte Bardot, Scarlett Speedwell, Ninivah, and Yves St Laurent. The ingenious advertising campaign featured photographs of the actor Leslie Phillips as a bowler-hatted and pinstripe-suited old fogey, walking along Jermyn Street and being amazed (perhaps not unpleasurably) by the sight of pretty girls and bronzed boys in their peacock clothing entering Simpsons. The inaugural reception included a fashion show compèred by Penelope Keith (with Earl Mountbatten as guest of honour - David Hicks was his son-in-law); the fashion shows were repeated in a series of public performances presented by Leslie Phillips. In the autumn, a popular series of fashion shows was presented by Prudence Glynn (Lady Windlesham), fashion editor of *The Times*; these were compèred by Derek Nimmo. The new Jermyn Street shop was designed by David Hicks to provide a setting resembling the drawing-room of an English country house. The corner shop on Church Place became a specifically DAKS shop, fitted out with armchairs in buttoned leather, and display shelving and furnishings of mahogany and brass similar to those in a traditional Pall Mall gentleman's club: DAKS Corner was opened by Gerald Harper.

At the same time, Johnny Mengers designed a DAKS check, incorporating the colours of camel and vicuna, two of the most luxurious and expensive fabrics, contrasted with black or (occasionally) white. These colours were carried into the packaging of Simpson Picadilly. A redecoration of the store was instituted, including the introduction of carpet covering the original cork floors - the carpet, naturally, woven in a tweed effect using the three colours of camel, vicuna and black. In addition, the style and colours were introduced into Simpson Piccadilly advertising in the increasing numbers of newspaper colour supplements. Lavish colour advertising was linked with brochures emphasising the British country style. In his promotion of DAKS, Johnny Mengers determined to reintroduce the original DAKS trouser. Having organised production, he set out to market them with a dramatic campaign using black-and-white photographs. Perhaps the greatest black-and-white fashion photographer of the Thirties, particularly in *Vogue*, was Horst P Horst. Simpson's advertising agent Vernon Stratton discovered that Horst

British Designers Exhibition at Simpsons and the Victoria & Albert Museum in 1979, designed by Peter Southgate:

Jean Muir - peach blouse;

Zandra Rhodes - dress and short cape in ultramarine;

Janice Wainwright - black jersey dress with gold trimmings;

Roland Klein - charcoal coat and silk printed dress.

was still working (in his eighties) at his home on Long Island, New York, and happy to be commissioned. A photographic session in New York produced a series of dramatic fashion pictures in black-and-white, with heavy shadow contrasts, accompanied by the slogan 'One look tells you it's the DAKS original from the 1930s'. This was followed by the introduction of a definitive DAKS aports jacket and DAKS blazer, accompanied by a new identity symbol of the 'double D'. The DAKS logo was added to the Piccadilly facade of the store. The DAKS blazer had a distinguished launch at the Commonwealth Games in Edmonton, Canada, when all the Federation officers wore a uniform of DAKS blazer and trousers - including the President of the Federation, the Duke of Edinburgh.

In that year also, a new subsidiary company, DAKS-Simpson (Far East) Limited, was incorporated. Johnny Mengers had pioneered a series of licensing agreements for the parent company, and that with Sankyo Seiko based in Osaka, Japan was proving particularly successful. The new 'traditional English' image of DAKS-Simpson appealed particularly to the Japanese market. Among the recipients of gold watches for 21 years' service to Simpson Piccadilly in 1978 was 'Mr Andrew' - Andrew Simeonidis - who had joined the store as an interpreter and become manager of the export department. Fluent in English, French, Italian, German, Greek and Arabic, he was 'currently learning Japanese'.

That summer [1978] a Riding and Country Shop was opened on the fifth floor, featuring riding coats marketed by Bernard Weatherill Limited, the London tailor (whose chairman was to become Speaker of the House of Commons). Simpson's public relations manager, Richard Campbell-Walter, arranged for a horse-box to be fitted out to take merchandise and fixtures to shows throughout the country, providing living accomodation for Simpson staff. This appeared for the first time at the International Horse Show at Wembley. It soon became a popular feature of all the leading riding events, such as Badminton, Burghley, Hickstead and Olympia.

The introduction of foreign brand names and merchandise into Simpson Piccadilly was certainly in the mainstream of young fashion. But it caused

Christmas windows by Peter Southgate with paintings by the Hon. Janet Kydd.

what might be called creative tension between the store and the parent company, since the latter was concerned to promote Britishness. There was an unhappy incident when a north-country wool manufacturer walked by chance into the new store, bought a suit that took his fancy and found when he got it home that it was made in Italy. Outraged, he wrote a blunt Yorkshire letter of complaint to Dr Simpson (asserting, among other things, that Royal Warrant Holders should not deal in foreign merchandise). Dr Simpson refunded his money and courteously explained that the new Store was only a part of the company's business, and that the parent company had a distinguished record in exporting British goods.

Simpson Piccadilly had often promoted special displays of British goods. At this period British fashion designers, many of them young, were creating a considerable impact worldwide. It was Dr Simpson's idea to invite a number of them to join together to present a major exhibition in the store. Coordinated by Barbara Griggs, fashion editor of the *Daily Mail*, the display was designed by Peter Southgate and occupied the whole of the third floor. Originally intended to last for one week, it attracted so much attention that it was extended for a second week. Many of the 25 participating designers were already internationally famous names - Jean Muir, Zandra Rhodes, Caroline Charles, Janice Wainwright, Bill Gibb, Roland Klein and Michiko. Others were final-year students or recent graduates from at the Royal College of Art. At the conclusion of the exhibition, at the suggestion of Margaret Box and through the generosity of the participating designers, the mannequin suppliers Adel Rootstein and the sculptor John Taylor, the whole display was given to the Victoria and Albert Museum, where it was re-staged in the Department of Dress for a further week. Accepting the gift, the Director of the V & A, Dr Roy Strong, said: 'Thanks to Simpson, we have been presented with a chunk of fashion history. I am thrilled - but the 2079 AD visitor will be even more so.'

Another aspect of British history was imaginatively illustrated by Simpsons that summer, when the racehorse Red Rum won the Grand National for the third time. Clippings from his hair were woven into a twist worsted for hacking jackets, which were woven in Scotland from a mixture of 95% wool, 4% camel hair and 1% Red Rum. The resulting jackets were displayed at Simpson Piccadilly. Yet another sport was celebrated when the Walter Hagen Cup was awarded (by the sports writers of America) to the British golfer Henry Cotton, who was presented with it by Dr Simpson at a reception in the store.

Attention having been attracted to Jermyn Street by the creation of the new Simpson shops, Dr Simpson realised that there was no association of the shopkeepers in that distinguished thoroughfare (considered so elegant when the store opened, that the local authority at first refused permission for the store to use neon display lighting on the facade, as being too

Johnny Mengers.

vulgar). So having approached all the shopkeepers in the street, the Jermyn Street Association was founded (and its members promptly elected Dr Simpson as its first chairman). That Christmas, the Association arranged for decorations to be strung along the street, and a Christmas tree was placed in the churchyard of St James's Piccadilly, the lights being switched on by Ernie Wise.

A new government had been elected in 1979 with Mrs Margaret Thatcher as Britain's first woman Prime Minister. It was a misfortune that because of international events the country was soon suffering the effects of a major recession, which adversely affected trade and led to rising unemployment. At Simpson Piccadilly, Martin Moss had been persuaded to return as managing director of the store and a director of the parent company S Simpson Limited, where Freddie Brame had retired as deputy chairman, to be succeeded by Johnny Mengers. The early years of the 1980s were to be challenging for both the parent company and the store.

Martin Moss decided that a major promotion was required to bring customers into the store, and to provide optimism and uplift at a challenging time. Assisted by the promotion expertise of Margaret Box, he planned a major exhibition with the title British Enterprise. It was staged throughout Simpson Piccadilly in September 1980, and was opened by the Rt Hon James Prior, then Secretary of State for Employment. Some sixty British companies agreed to take part, and there were sufficient exhibits to provide interesting displays on each floor of the store. Together with a substantial DAKS promotion were stands from, among others, Anglia Television, Aston Martin, British Aerospace, British Airways, British Gas, British Leyland, British Rail, British Telecom, Chubb & Son, Cranfield Institute of Technology, the Design Council, the Ministry of Defence, General Electric Company, Goldsmiths Company, International Computers, JCB Sales, Lansing, Lotus Cars, Lucas Industries, Marconi, National Coal Board, Plessey Avionics, the Post Office, Rediffusion, Rolls Royce Aero Engines, Royal College of Art, Royal Society of Arts, Royal Ordnance

Leslie Parker, Dr Leonard Simpson and Martin Moss.

Factories, Short Brothers, Standard Telephones & Cables, Tube Investments, Vickers Instruments and Medical, and Westland Helicopters. It was a remarkable exhibition, putting leading British companies on public show in the heart of London at a troublesome time.

The continuing recession in the early years of the eighties led to inflation, rising prices and declining sales. Simpson Piccadilly was no more able to escape the cold wind than all other retail stores. It was a difficult period, despite efforts to expand advertising and give the store a still more vigorous image. A series of 'advertorials' were devised, sharing sponsorship with appropriate manfacturers in the luxury market, and using dramatic photography by Albert Watson of New York. These created considerable impact when they appeared in *Vogue* and *Harpers/Queen*. An arrangement was reached with *Vogue* whereby the magazine would direct and present a November issue including a section on Simpson Piccadilly and its associate manufacturers, which was then run-on for distribution to customers as the store's Christmas catalogue. In the same period, Martin Moss commissioned a re-design of the Piccadilly entrance and the ground floor of the store. This was designed by Maurice Broughton, who admired Joseph Emberton's architecture and produced a sympathetic result that not only returned the entrance more nearly to what Emberton had originally intended (though adding wind-proof glass screens), but enabled the first area of the store seen by customers to be converted to a series of small speciality boutiques, initially for cosmetics.

In 1982 Jack Creed retired, after 12 years as a director of Simpson Piccadilly, and six years as joint deputy managing director. Dynamic, a salesman to his fingertips, he made it his business to meet and greet as many customers as possible, many of whom became personal friends (among them Prince Rainier, who when visiting London would often call in to shop at Simpsons, often with his family). Jack Creed was as friendly to the ordinary customer as to the famous, though many found that somehow his delight in showing them attractive merchandise meant that they left the store having bought rather more than they had intended. From the ground floor, he gradually became super-salesman for the entire store, and was one of those mainly responsible for rebuilding the business of Simpson Piccadilly after the lean years of the war. On Jack Creed's retirement, two other directors were appointed: Sally Hunter, a distinguished and effective fashion director, and Richard Campbell-Walter, an imaginative and creative director of public relations.

In 1982 Simpson Piccadilly received its third Royal Warrant of Appointment, that of HRH The Prince of Wales.

Dr S Leonard Simpson died at his home in Sussex on 3 August 1983 at the age of 82. His death saddened people in the many spheres of life to which he had contributed so much dedication and care: medicine, retailing, sport and the arts (he had been a skilled painter in watercolour and oils). A memorial service at St James's Church Piccadilly, held in December, was conducted by the Rector, the Revd. Donald Reeves, and his precedessor, the Very Revd. William Baddeley. There were addresses by Professor Victor Wynn (Dr Simpson's colleague at St Mary's Hospital, Paddington), and Michael Denison. Penelope Keith, Christopher Biggins, Dulcie Gray and Anthony Andrews read poems. Douglas Bunn of Hickstead read a lesson, recalling Dr Simpson's love of many forms of sport; another lesson was read by Leslie Parker, representing the Simpson group of companies and Simpson Piccadilly. Moura Lympany played some of Dr

Dr Leonard Simpson.

Simpson's favourite pieces. Then, in farewell, Patricia Hodge in white tie and tails, with top hat and cane, sang the Edwardian song that so epitomised Piccadilly, 'Burlington Bertie' - at the end, dancing quietly away so that the song faded to a whisper. It was a touch, everyone agreed, that would have delighted 'Doctor'.

In his memory, the family and the company provided a substantial additional endowment for the medical research laboratory at St Mary's Hospital which had originally been founded in 1964 by Dr Simpson in memory of his brother, the creator of Simpson Piccadilly (and was shortly

British Enterprise Exhibition, store facade;

British Airways Concorde;

British Cars - Triumph TR7, Lagonda, Scimitar.

afterwards visited by Princess Margaret). It was thereafter renamed the Alexander and Leonard Simpson Laboratory for Metabolic Research.

Only a few weeks after Dr Simpson's memorial service, Frederick Brame died at the age of 75, four years after his retirement from the board of S Simpson Limited, the parent company. He had truly given his life to the company, and to the store. He had first joined Simpsons straight from school, as a clerk in the office of the Stoke Newington factory. He had soon been noticed by Alec Simpson, who recognised his quickness of mind, his skill with figures (a great attribute in the days before electronic calculators), and his total trustworthiness. Though he had not been closely involved with the building of Simpson Piccadilly, when the store faced challenging times in the months following the opening it was Freddie Brame, then only 28, whom Alec Simpson drafted in as company secretary of the store, to apply his clarity and discipline to its administration.

Freddie Brame remained at Piccadilly throughout the war, and was appointed a director in 1944. He became managing director in 1959 and deputy chairman in 1964. For more than half a century he was Dr Simpson's right-hand, first in the administration of Simpson Piccadilly, and latterly of the parent company (of which he was deputy chairman from 1966-80, finally retiring from the board in 1981). He was a Christian gentleman, a devoted Baptist, who while blessed with a close-knit family life spent considerable time and effort in the service of the Boys' Brigade in his home area of Waltham Forest, where he was President of the local Battalion for ten years. He later became instrumental in raising finance to provide the Brigade with a national headquarters, and was appointed an Honorary Vice-President. He was a keen cricketer in his young days, an enthusiastic golfer, and an active figure in the Simpson Social Club. A gregarious man, he had a table permanently booked in the store restaurant, and there was scarcely a day when he was not being host to business associates over lunch. All in the store recognised that his often-repeated quotation that 'where there is no vision the people perish' was exemplified throughout his service to Simpsons.

He put his philosophy into words when invited in 1970 to speak on retailing at the London School of Economics and the London Graduate School of Business Studies.

Noting that 'success in retailing is firmly based on the twin pillars of Staff and Stock', he went on to speak of fashion.

In its trading policy Simpson (Piccadilly) Limited is a fashion and trend-setting store . . . There are, of course, basic principles which govern trends in consumer demand - in all consumer demands which stem from the generation in which we live, the tradition of the past and the aspirations and fears of the future.

Putting it another way, one can say that trends in consumer demand are due fundamentally to the political, economic and social order of our life. These three headings are often, in themselves, so closely interwoven that it is sometimes difficult to define where the political ends and the economic begins, or where the economic starts and the social takes over.

Merchandising has a more practical application as it demands that modern technical progress in the field of textile machinery must be studied and, in particular, there must be knowledge and understanding of the revolutionary developments taking place in the construction of synthetic and mixture fibres and . . . an awareness of the enormous influence now exercised by the younger generation on fashion and trend in its widest and fullest sense.

The marketing team, on the other hand, is composed of specialists whose whole effort is centred on every aspect of selling . . . In this field one brings together the creative ability of the display staff with the promotional know-how of the advertising team and the organising ability of the Store Marketing Manager and those responsible for each specialist department.

Simpson Piccadilly is not a large store . . . It is, therefore, still very much a personal business and by constant collaboration the good relationship between the merchandising and marketing teams can be maintained.

Dr Simpson was succeeded as chairman of the Simpson group of companies, and of Simpson (Piccadilly) Limited, by Johnny Mengers. He was keen to increase the public profile of DAKS still further, and believed that the store should become primarily an outlet for the products of the manufacturing company DAKS-Simpson Limited. Martin Moss chose to leave the company to head National Trust Enterprises: he was succeeded at the end of 1984 as managing director of Simpson Piccadilly by Jeremy Franks. Mr Franks, who began his career on the international sales side of the woollens trade, then moved to the up-market tie trade, had been for some years the representative in Canada of a leading British clothing manufacturer. Fluent in French and German, he was therefore well experienced in the markets served by what had now become the DAKS Simpson Group.

DAKS slacks updated to 1990 and photographed by Horst. The novelty of the high rise waist, reverse front pleats and patent waist adjustment made them an immediate sell-out.

THE EIGHTIES

1986: Golden Jubilee year, celebrated on the seashore at Camber Sands. Timeless fashions, styled by Liz Tilberis and photographed by Alex Chatelain; Roland Klein and (next page) Armani suit and the dress by Designing Women.

Roland Klein at Simpson Piccadilly

The ups and downs of fashion. (left) 1985: a long line suit by Roland Klein in pleated polyester, which had just re-entered fashion thanks to its silky handle and permanent pleatability; a 1990 jacket and skirt with the square shoulder, a feature of the mid 1980s and introduced by Versace.

1983: the quintessential 1980s look, photographed by John Bishop. (l-r) a typically understated Jean Muir dress, Armani suit, and a sexy Emanuel Little Black Dress, all from International Fashion.

High or rather low romance in a traditional party frock from Judy Mott, 1988. Full puff sleeves had been a formal fashion staple ever since the Princess of Wales, Emanuel wedding dress of 1981. (Right) The sleek alternative from the Georgina Simpson collection of young style fashion, 1984. Lingerie, 1988, was luxuriously traditional.

Overleaf, 1984: quality cotton dresses; (1-r) Simpson exclusives, Dejac, Pisanti. They are easy fitting but unmistakably stylish with their bulky square shoulders and high cut necklines. Vernon Stratton, the advertising agency staged the photograph on location at Sandown, Isle of Wight. It was styled by Tony Chettle and photographed by Graham Hughes. It is almost a first appearance of the third royal warrant, that of the Prince of Wales awarded in 1982, to join that of the Queen, 1962 and the Duke of Edinburgh, 1956.

THE EIGHTIES

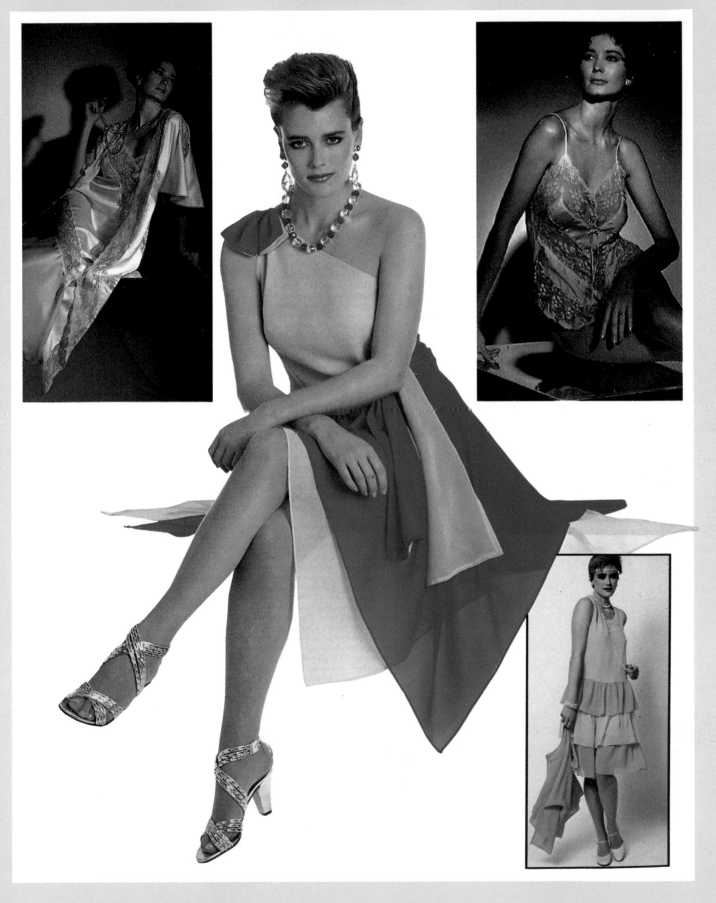

By 1981 men's fashion was on the straight and losing the narrow. The fit and flare so characteristic of the 1970s has gone, the jacket waist had dropped and the shoulder line was looser and less wide, balanced by a longer lapel and a less exaggerated shirt and tie. Trousers were straight cut. (1-r) a s.b. lounge suit, a d.b. lounge suit, a dinner jacket. By 1986 (bottom 1-r) especially for easy fitting country and travel wear, the line had relaxed still further and the jacket hangs almost straight from the shoulder. Tweeds were the ultimate in export success. For the Dutch market, in the new just invented Daks check, a sports jacket, and for her an ensuite set of walking shorts, bag and Baker Boy cap. For the possibly more conservative Swiss market, an easy fitting suit, with looser longer jacket and easy fitting length skirt.

(bottom r and opposite): **By the early 1980s**, exercise and the sporting life were a universal agenda. For golf, 1980, there was an outfit non specific in style though specified in content, with a Daks check hat, an Allen Solly cotton shirt, a needle cord suit by Invertère, over boxer shorts by Sunspel with desert boots by Atkinson and socks by Viyella. Trolley and bag were also available from Simpson.

THE EIGHTIES

(*continued from page opposite*) More forward looking are the cycling clothes, 1983, cotton and acrylic polo shirts from Alan Paige with easy fitting cotton pants. Tennis, from the Wimbledon programme, 1982, was still traditional, and ski wear, by Head of Germany, 1986, had moved into the space age.

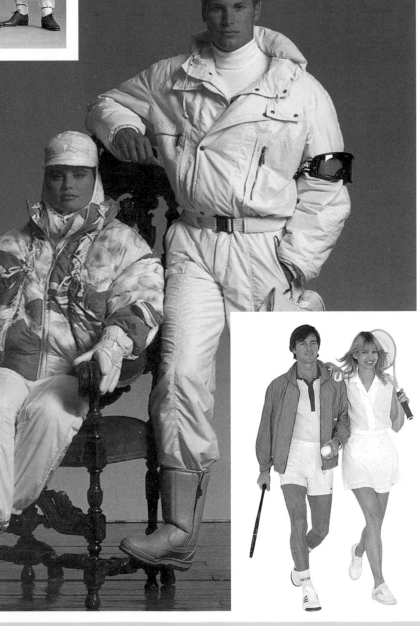

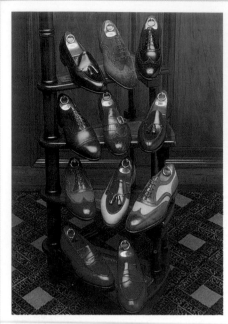

Simpson catalogues had promoted predictable and high quality fashion by post since the 1930s. Many items remained in the range through the decades as staples of Simpson style such as Viyella shirts there since the 1930s and Glaser jersey suits from Switzerland, everyday understated fashion since the 1960s, and as always the blazer jacket…

(l-r): shoes, 1989-90; man's outfit 1987; holiday weekend outfit, 1988; jackets and skirts, 1991; Viyella shirts, 1987, though here city stripe not country check; (below) woman's outfits 1987. Glaser suits, 1991.

NIGHTWEAR IN PURE COTTON BY DEREK ROSE

(a) Striped nightshirt in red with navy, also available in yellow with navy or emerald with navy, sizes S, M, L, XL, £35.
(b) Plain navy pyjamas with self satin stripe and emerald piping, also available in red with navy piping or yellow with navy piping, sizes 38-46, £52.
(c) Striped dressing gown in navy with emerald, also available in navy with yellow or navy with red, sizes M, L, XL, £65.
(d) Patchwork striped nightshirt in yellow with navy, also available in red with navy or emerald with navy, sizes S, M, L, XL, £35.
(e) Red and navy striped pyjamas, also available in emerald with navy or yellow with navy, sizes 38-46, £45.
(f) Striped dressing gown in navy with red, also available in navy with emerald or navy with yellow, sizes M, L, XL, £65.

19

7

FRESH DIRECTIONS

The Golden Jubilee of Simpson Piccadilly was celebrated in style on the evening of 29th April 1986. In a triumph of organisation, the store traded normally until 5.30 pm, at which time it closed to the public and a small army of staff began an almost total clearance of three floors. By 7 o'clock, the ground floor was filling with many of the 600 guests who had eagerly snapped up tickets for what was certainly one of the most glittering events in the West End. Soon afterwards, the principal guest, HRH The Princess Royal, arrived accompanied by Captain Mark Phillips. Princess Anne honoured the party in her capacity as President of the Save the Children Fund, for whose benefit the occasion was held; Captain Phillips was familiar with Simpson Piccadilly and its parent company, DAKS Simpson, in connection with show jumping promotions: the company had also for many years supported the Pony Club.

With the arrival of the final guests, the party moved up to the second floor, where a fashion show was presented, the final scene of which was entirely modelled by celebrities from the West End theatres. A tombola was drawn, with Michael Parkinson acting as Master of Ceremonies. Following that, everyone moved up to the third floor where dinner was set for 600. At the end of the meal, and the cutting of Simpson Piccadilly 50th birthday cake, Mrs Georgina Andrews presented to Princess Anne a cheque for £56,000, the amount raised by the party for the Save the Children Fund. A cabaret was then presented by Billy Connolly. That was not the end of the occasion, for on the second floor the setting of the fashion show had been replaced by Stringfellows' disco, to whose music many guests stayed to dance into the early hours.

This evening marking the Store's Golden Jubilee was a 'one-off', and a memorable success, not least because of the large number of people who could comfortably be entertained in the building. But the store was accustomed to hosting events with large attendances from time to time. In the last week of November in each year the Royal Yachting Association holds a buffet dinner in the store, during its International Conference week. The entire lower ground floor is transformed into a restaurant for the occasion, and among the guests have been the late King Olav of Norway and King Constantine of Greece.

In 1988 Leslie Parker retired after ten years as deputy managing director. He had been a loyal lieutenant to Freddie Brame, and in the most difficult years as well as the more profitable had followed his mentor by ensuring that the store's accounts were kept with rigorous precision, and that the financial stability of Simpson Piccadilly remained sound (he had been succeeded as company secretary by Colin Campbell in 1984). One of his greatest services was successfully to conduct the long negotiations that enabled the store to expand along Jermyn Street. Leslie Parker chose to

Store fascia for the Japanese promotion, 1989
(by Michael Bentley, display executive);

Japanese kite in the Men's Department;

Japanese water garden;

Japanese Air Lines lanterns suspended in the
Store's stair-well;

Window using Japanese screens and kimono.

Opposite:

HRH The Princess Anne is introduced to Mrs
Heddy Simpson by Jeremy Franks, managing
director;

Princess Anne with Michael Caine;

Betty Kenward, doyenne of the West End's social
columnists, arriving at Simpson Piccadilly, with
racing driver Jackie Stewart;

Anthony and Georgina Andrews.

retire shortly before Christmas, a busy time for the store: and when he was
told that his friend the general manager of Claridge's had invited him to
lunch there, he sent a message that he was grateful for the thought, but
was far too busy. Fortunately he was persuaded, grumbling, to go; that was
fortunate, since he discovered that his wife and some sixty of his business
friends and associates in the West End had assembled to honour him. He
did not seriously retire, except from his day-to-day responsibilities in
Simpson Piccadilly, since he became consultant to the DAKS Simpson
group. Subsequently he became director of the British Menswear Guild (of
which Jeremy Franks became chairman in 1991).

In 1989 the store mounted a substantial Japanese promotion, and
Simpson Piccadilly was dressed throughout in the best of traditional and
modern Japanese design. This promotion was mounted in association with
the parent company's Japanese licensees, Sankyo Seiko, and was a
recognition of the increasing importance of the business links between
Britain and the trading power of the Pacific Rim.

The association of the Simpson family with the store, a matter of
profound importance to the inheritors of the family name, became deeply
significant when in 1990 the DAKS Simpson Group of companies, including
Simpson (Piccadilly) Limited, received a takeover bid from the Sankyo
Seiko group, based in Osaka, Japan. This company had for 20 years been
DAKS licensees in Japan. The sum offered was £65 million. Naturally the
family shareholders, led by Mrs Heddy Simpson, her daughter Mrs
Georgina Andrews and half-brother Johnny Mengers, considered the
proposition for some months before deciding that it would be in the
interest of the Simpson business, and also of the store, to accept a bid that
would guarantee its future within a well-found company that had long
been associated with the DAKS Simpson Group and was very familiar with
its products (from 1988 to 1990 the sales of DAKS products in Japan had
risen from 18.6 billion Yen to 23 billion Yen). The family shareholders left
the business on the acceptance of the takeover in February 1991, but not

Hideo Miki.

Jeremy Franks.

before Mrs Georgina Andrews had visited the store to talk to the staff, thank them for their service to the Simpson family over the years, and wish them good fortune in the future (Mrs Heddy Simpson died in November 1994: she was remembered for her keen interest in the store, and the inventiveness of her flow of ideas on its fashion direction; her obituarists recalled her as 'a unique lady greatly missed by her family and many friends'.)

Jeremy Franks became chief executive and managing director of DAKS Simpson Group PLC, and joined the board of Sankyo Seiko Co. Limited, Japan, under the Presidency of Hideo Miki. Planning of the future development of the DAKS Simpson Group commenced.

Plans were already well advanced for the celebration of the centenary of the House of Simpson, which took place in 1994. The store was appropriately decorated, special packaging produced for the year, and a book (*The House that DAKS Built*) published and a video (*Seeking Perfection*) produced to record the 100 years since Simeon Simpson began his bespoke tailoring business in Middlesex Street in the City of London. A number of the company's landmarks were illustrated: the building of a great factory in Stoke Newington in the 1920s, and the subsequent transfer of production to Scotland (where the Larkhall factory was visited by the Queen, accompanied by the Duke of Edinburgh, in 1979). The development of licensing worldwide, but particularly in the Far East, was described. So was the introduction by Johnny Mengers of a Group identity, worked through in many different presentations: colours, the DAKS typography, tartans, and a 'double-D' logo. All these were certainly right for the time. The Store had been partially refurbished as resources allowed (the original cork flooring, with rugs, had been covered with carpet woven in the DAKS colours of camel, vicuna and black; and in 1987 the handrail of the main staircase, having become badly worn after 50 years, had been re-enamelled in colours carefully matched as closely as possible to the original; in 1994 the coloured neon lighting of the Piccadilly facade was restored to a new brilliance).

The 'Corner Shop' in Jermyn Street had been redesigned as the 'Studio' shop for the younger man, using one of the oldest Simpson logos - the needle-and-thread 'S', with the letter formed by a flowing thread curling round a needle (the logo dated back at least to the Twenties, and perhaps earlier). The 'Studio' line was a softer, relaxed tailoring collection featuring linen, cotton and silk mix jackets, trousers, waistcoats and suits.

Simpson Piccadilly continued to be, as it was planned to be, a West End showroom for the products of the DAKS-Simpson Group. But it was also, as it was planned to be, a showroom for the most innovative and interesting merchandise from around the world, a place where a man could be kitted out in one store, in formal or country wear, with sportswear appropriate to the season. Within the Store, therefore, could be found many of the world's most fashionable names: in the early 90s, Paul Costelloe, Valentino, Guy Laroche, Armani, Marlboro Classics, Cerruti Brothers, Mulberry; Calvin Klein underwear, Armani underwear and nightwear, and ties from Duchamp, Kenzo, DAKS and Cerruti. For women, in 1995, there were collections from Genny Way, Studio Ferre, Yves St Laurent and Guy Laroche, with leisure and casualwear from Mulberry and Armani swimwear, with collections from Weekend by Max Mara and Armani Jeans. There were also concessionaires within the store: the Jermyn Street section of the store was transformed into a Joseph shop for the younger

Malcolm Busby.

Ground floor of the store for Ireland Today.

woman, with its own restaurant; next door (behind a red door) was an Elizabeth Arden shop. (The store's main restaurant on the lower ground floor now featured a Sushi bar: originally introduced as a one-week promotion, it soon became a popular meeting-place for Japanese visitors to London.) The barber's shop on the lower ground floor was now Trumper's; Church's Shoes ran their own shop; as did Leonardi's Chocolates.

With promotion of Jeremy Franks to run the DAKS Simpson Group, it was decided to seek for the store a manager with a background in retailing. Malcolm Busby was appointed retail director of the store in April 1992, and managing director of Simpson Piccadilly in 1994. His experience was that of a retailer and shopkeeper, having trained with the John Lewis Partnership and Harrods.

The new owners appreciated the respect for tradition that inspired the DAKS Simpson Group. It was recognised that, by the regular flow of fashion, open uncluttered sales floors and imaginative presentation of goods were once more becoming the admired style in international marketing. It was accepted that the combination of 'stock and staff' was the most vital element of the success of Simpson Piccadilly. The most fashionable and modern merchandise must be presented with the highest standard of service, which is known to managers as 'total quality management'. These were the rules by which Alexander Simpson had planned the store, and which applied as much in the last decade of the century as in 1936.

The imaginative vigour of the store's promotions continued to be in evidence, as demonstrated in the windows and displays. One of the happiest coincidences was when a major promotion of merchandise from Ireland was mounted in October 1994 under the title Ireland Today. It happened to coincide with the cessation of violence in Northern Ireland, and became in some sense a celebration of the probable increase in trade between the neighbouring communities.

In discussions on the long-term future of the store, it was agreed that development should be carried out one step at a time, and that improvements should be made on a long-term investment plan. Of course it is accepted in Japan as in Great Britain that the memory of the Second World War presents unavoidable historical tensions and human feelings, particularly among older people, that must be respected. These matters of history are fully understood, and the past must be honoured. But life moves forward, and it is the intention of the present directors that the best people should be appointed to carry the business onward positively and creatively, and that the modern managers should be provided with the authority and resources to succeed in this, in an atmosphere of openness and common respect.

Simpson Piccadilly has always faced challenges. Though a much admired modern building (in 1987 it was designated a 'structural steel classic' by the British Steel Corporation) its site, though within sight of Piccadilly Circus, one of the most famous and visited tourist sites in the world, is not on a street devoted solely to shopping. Piccadilly has famous hotels and clubs, internationally famed art galleries, and the offices of national and airline travel organisations. Stores in such a situation have to make particular efforts to attract customers. This has been recognised throughout the life of Simpson Piccadilly by the flair devoted to special promotions - such as the Japanese promotion in 1989, the Ireland Today promotion in 1994, and the imaginative dressing of the store's windows on

Piccadilly and Jermyn Street, a notable feature of the Store throughout sixty years. Indeed, when the London *Evening Standard* ran a competition for window display in London stores, it was won for the first two years by Simpson Piccadilly. In the third year, Simpsons decided not to enter, in order to give other participants a chance: the *Evening Standard* invited Michael Bentley, the display executive of Simpson Piccadilly, to join the judging panel.

In 1995 a major refurbishment of the store was begun, with the ready agreement of its present owners. The store scarcely needs structural modernisation, since it has been a flagship of modernity from the day it opened. But inevitably parts of the structure and areas of the store were starting to show their age, after nearly 60 years. They needed the tonic of refurbishment, to renew the freshness and vigour so characteristic of Simpson Piccadilly. The wheel has come full circle, and the Store will once more sparkle with the energy and excitement of its early days. Properly proud of its traditional high standards of service, Simpson Piccadilly sets out on its next 60 years reinvigorated, offering its customers of all generations and backgrounds, from Britain and from abroad, the best and most innovative examples of modern styling in men's and women's clothing and accessories.

Ireland Today promotion, October 1994 and other recent window displays.

Classic fashion photographer of the 1930s Horst P Horst updated a romantic retrospection of 1930s Daks fashion into an authorative statement for the late 1980s with his series entitled "One look tells you its the Daks original…" 50 years on, the images have been given a look of suave sophistication as seductive to 90s clients as had been jaunty practical optimism in the 30s. Little was changed though perhaps the shoulders were a less squared and the high peaked lapels a little longer. A woman in a man's world: extremely popular with the clients but not to appear in the updated range.

A double breasted lounge suit and, bottom right, a blazer from the Horst 1990 series.

1991: and the suit begins to shape up for the 1990s. Still easy fitting at the shoulder, the jackets are losing some of their fullness. The stronger vertical line of the SB suit is confirmed by the tight pinned shirt collar and the neat tie, also to be seen in the Horst picture. Trousers are an easy fit straight cut with pleats at the waist. The photographs, with the Simpson prize winning 1934 Concourse Bentley, are by Alexandre Cabreira.

(top) **The Daks Range, 1990,** combines classic styling with modish colour accents. Opulent clothes in line with the optimistic '80s. The blazer jacket and matching waistcoat recall Edwardian styles. They are bound in the company colours and on the pocket is the 1985 Daks badge, a coat of arms which in its quartering commemorates the City of London and Middlesex Street, the site of Simeon Simpson's first workshop, Scotland, where the present factory is situated, the mailed fist for man's clothing issuing from a crown of excellence grasping the world and its market.

(bottom) **1992 and easy fitting American golf styling** is suggested for an ever increasing Japanese clientele. The clothes have more to offer the serious golfer than the constricting semi sports wear of the 1980s. An informal jacket in which Coatwright, Invertère, established 1904 and taken over by Simpson in 1962, add a touch of native American trim to their "Authentic and Traditional English designed Sports and Weatherwear".

(opposite): **1990 and Michelle Brooks wears an easy fitting man styled Daks jacket** with suede trousers and waistcoat. The button loop at the collar had not been featured since 1930s men's sports coats. Below, 1991, a long line suit with velvet beret.

1991 and definitive fashion with a Christian Dior Coordonnes suit, with a defined and fitted jacket and one of the new shorter skirts. The hat is by Frederick Fox. The informally formal by US Diane Freis, in beaded silk chiffon, and her luxury bathing suit.

1991: the International Designer
collection reintroduces André Courrèges in an exclusive up to the minute replay of his classic 1960s space age styling: a zip front duffle jacket over lycra leggings and turtle neck top.

THE NINETIES

(opposite): **The best selling suit of 1990** by Morrice DaQuin of Paris, in extrovert yet classic styling.

Where next? Classic styling for 1995-6 India Hicks in traditional Daks jacket and jeans; a Sahza jacket with long line skirt; an Amanda Woodward range, new for 1996 with the characteristic long shapely jacket.

SOURCES

Bauhaus 50 years, Catalogue of an Exhibition sponsored by the Federal Republic of Germany at the Royal Academy of Arts, London, 1968

Brame, Frederick, *The Development & Organisation of Simpson (Piccadilly) Ltd.*, Paper given to the London School of Economics and the London Graduate School of Business Studies, London, privately printed, 1970

Gill, Eric, *Clothes an essay upon the nature and significance of the natural and artificial integuments worn by men and women*, London, Jonathan Cape, 1931

Havinden, Ashley, RDI FSIA, *Advertising and Commercial Design*, Cantor Lecture delivered at the Royal Society of Arts 17 November 1947, London, Journal of the RSA, 30 Jan 1948

Hitchcock, Henry Russell, *Architecture, Nineteenth and Twentieth Centuries*, The Pelican History of Art, Harmondsworth, 1958

Ind, Rosemary, *Emberton*, London and Berkeley, Scolar Press, 1983

Industrial Arts, quarterly journal, Summer issue, London, 1936

Jefferys, James B, *Retail Trading in Britain* 1850-1950, (National Institute of Economic and Social Research, Economic Studies XIII), Cambridge University Press, 1954

Kroll, Natasha, RDI FSIAD, *Window Display*, Studio Books, London, 1954

L Moholy-Nagy, Catalogue of an Exhibition arranged by the Arts Council of Great Britain, Institute of Contemporary Arts, London, 1980

Lawrence, A W (ed.), *T E Lawrence by his friends* (contribution by R G Sims), Jonathan Cape, London, 1937

Moholy-Nagy, László, *The New Vision* (1928, 4th ed 1947) (translated from the German by Daphne M Hoffman) and *Abstract of an Artist*, New York, George Wittenborn, 1967

Pevsner, Nikolaus, *The Buildings of England, London 1, the Cities of London and Westminster*, London, Penguin, 1957

Saxon Mills, G H, *There is a Tide . . . The Life and Work of Sir William Crawford KBE*, embodying an historical study of modern British advertising, London, Heinemann, 1954

Thirties, British Art and Design before the War, Catalogue of an Exhibition organised by the Arts Council of Great Britain in collaboration with the Victoria & Albert Museum, London, 1979

The past with a future, fashion drawings by Eric Stemp, about 1970.

INDEX

PAUL HUGHES

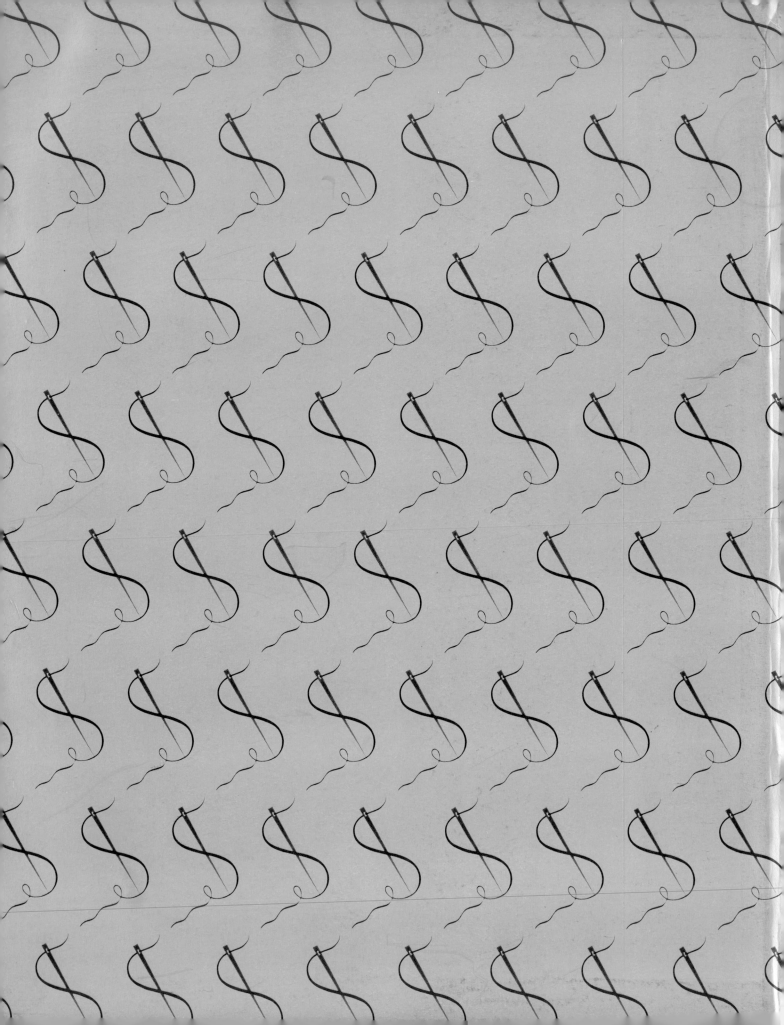